Ludwig Tieck and America

UNC | COLLEGE OF ARTS AND SCIENCES
Germanic and Slavic Languages and Literatures

From 1949 to 2004, UNC Press and the UNC Department of Germanic & Slavic Languages and Literatures published the UNC Studies in the Germanic Languages and Literatures series. Monographs, anthologies, and critical editions in the series covered an array of topics including medieval and modern literature, theater, linguistics, philology, onomastics, and the history of ideas. Through the generous support of the National Endowment for the Humanities and the Andrew W. Mellon Foundation, books in the series have been reissued in new paperback and open access digital editions. For a complete list of books visit www.uncpress.org.

Ludwig Tieck and America

PERCY MATENKO

UNC Studies in the Germanic Languages and Literatures
Number 12

Copyright © 1954

This work is licensed under a Creative Commons CC BY-NC-ND license. To view a copy of the license, visit http://creativecommons.org/licenses.

Suggested citation: Matenko, Percy. *Ludwig Tieck and America*. Chapel Hill: University of North Carolina Press, 1954. DOI: https://doi.org/10.5149/9781469657929_Matenko

Library of Congress Cataloging-in-Publication Data
Names: Matenko, Percy.
Title: Ludwig Tieck and America / by Percy Matenko.
Other titles: University of North Carolina Studies in the Germanic Languages and Literatures ; no. 12.
Description: Chapel Hill : University of North Carolina Press, [1954] Series: University of North Carolina Studies in the Germanic Languages and Literatures.
Identifiers: LCCN 54062860 | ISBN 978-1-4696-5791-2 (pbk: alk. paper) | ISBN 978-1-4696-5792-9 (ebook)
Subjects: Tieck, Ludwig, 1773-1853. | Comparative literature — German and American. | Comparative literature — American and German.
Classification: LCC PD25 .N6 NO. 12

Table of Contents

	PAGE
PREFACE	ix

CHAPTER ONE

    American Visitors and Tieck; Charles Follen 1

CHAPTER TWO

    Tieck's Reception in American Magazines and Books Prior to 1900

    A. Tieck's Reception in American Magazines Prior to 1900 13

    B. Tieck's Reception in American Books and Text Books Prior to 1900 29

CHAPTER THREE

    American Translations of Tieck 38

CHAPTER FOUR

    Tieck and American Authors 48

CHAPTER FIVE

    Tieck, Poe and Hawthorne 71

CHAPTER SIX

    Tieck's Attitude to America 89

CONCLUSIONS 92

APPENDIX

    A List of American Books in Tieck's Library According to the Asher Catalog of 1849 97

BIBLIOGRAPHY 107

INDEX 116

PREFACE

The rôle of Ludwig Tieck (1773-1853) in German literature is both remarkable and unique. It is difficult to overestimate the influence that this highly gifted and versatile man exerted as a creative writer, as a critic, dramaturgist and theoretician, as an editor and translator, as a stimulator and adviser of others. Twice in his long life he became a leader in new movements: among the early German romanticists in 1797; and, twenty years later, in the reaction against the fading and enervated romantic movement whose excesses he clearly recognized. He is the originator of the *Kunstmärchen*. And the use of romantic irony in his satirical dramas with fairytale motifs further attests his originality. The German theater profited much from his valuable criticism and advice. And German literature owes him a great deal for his publication of the works of Kleist, Novalis, Lenz, and Solger, some of which might otherwise have been lost to posterity. While Tieck could not be counted among the greatest German poets, he was a master of prose style. Kings honored him and Goethe esteemed him highly as a writer and as a dramaturgist. That the influence of such a man should extend far beyond the German-speaking world is a matter of course.

Because of the important rôle which Ludwig Tieck played in the German romantic movement, a study of Tieck and America up to 1900 should throw light on the reception in America of German romanticism as a whole.

Studies have been made of certain aspects of this subject, such as the relation between Tieck and Ticknor, and between Tieck and Washington Irving. Some work was also done by Goodnight and Haertel as part of their investigation of German literature in American magazines prior to 1846, and from 1846 to 1880, and in research on different phases of the Tieck-Poe and Tieck-Hawthorne relationship. But no attempt has as yet been made to study this problem in its entirety. It is this aim that I have sought to accomplish.

When my research began in 1944, it at once became clear that there were two phases to the problem: the influence of America on Tieck and the influence of Tieck on America. Further study showed that the importance of the second phase was greater than that of the first. The influence of America on Tieck, except for his library, was rather negative, and, considering the extent of his productivity, slight. The influence of Tieck on America, however, has been very considerable, and it can best be measured by studying its various aspects: visits by distinguished Americans to Tieck as well as references and reactions to him by Americans who visited Europe; his influence on Charles Follen; Tieck's reception in American magazines and his influence as it appears in various books and school editions prior to 1900; American translations of his works; his bearing on various American authors; the rather complicated relation between Tieck, Poe, and Hawthorne; and Tieck's attitude toward America. Each of these aspects has been treated in a separate chapter. Much can be said about Tieck's reception in America since 1900. It is, however, confined to academic, chiefly Germanistic, circles and falls outside the *terminus ad quem* of this study.

There are no footnotes in the text of this book because of the extensive source material given in my bibliography. This, I feel, can serve as a substitute, avoiding the duplication which would arise if footnotes were retained. I am convinced that most readers are not interested in the customary "*op. cit.'s*" and "*ibid.'s*," and I have therefore decided to dispense with most of them. I would be glad to furnish exact page references to any one requesting them on any point or question in my text.

It is my pleasant duty to acknowledge those who have assisted me in my work: Professor Robert Herndon Fife, Professor Emeritus of Columbia University and, particularly, Professor Edwin H. Zeydel of the University of Cincinnati, who has given me constant support, valuable constructive criticism, and encouragement throughout the course of the study; Professor Max I. Baym of the Polytechnic Institute of Brooklyn for his assistance as collaborator during the initial stage of this study; Professor Henry Zylstra for some useful suggestions and for permission to examine his unpublished dissertation; and Professors Mabbott and Henry A. Pochmann for valuable correspondence. A special debt of gratitude is due to the late Professor Henry Wadsworth Longfellow Dana for his many courtesies and very helpful advice while I was working at the Longfellow House, Cambridge, as well as later in connection with the study of the Tieck-Longfellow relationship. I am also indebted to him and to Miss Anne Longfellow Thorp for their kind permission to consult manuscript material there. For reading the manuscript and for constructive criticism I am indebted to my colleague of the English Department, and Assistant Director of the School of General Studies, Professor Bernard H. Stern. For services beyond their general facilities, I am indebted to the following libraries and archives: Columbia University for use of material from its divisions of special collections; Toronto University Library and Brooklyn College Library for making unpublished dissertations as well as rare books accessible through inter-library loan; the New York Forty-Second Street Library for use of its manuscript and rare book divisions and for various photostating services; and the Pierpont Morgan Library of New York for permission to examine manuscript material in its possession pertaining to Hawthorne and Tieck.

CHAPTER ONE

AMERICAN VISITORS AND TIECK; CHARLES FOLLEN

It is now an acknowledged fact that Ludwig Tieck was interested in and himself influenced the literary life of France, Denmark, England and Russia. Zeydel has devoted a whole monograph to a study of Tieck and England, and his book, *Ludwig Tieck, The German Romanticist,* provides evidence of Tieck's influence on other countries. Tieck's relation to America has also been explored, but only with regard to certain aspects of his influence, as referred to below. The present study seeks to deal with the subject in its entirety.

One of the most significant aspects of Tieck and America is the record of visits by distinguished Americans to Tieck, or reactions to Tieck by Americans who visited Europe. To this influence should be added the impression that Tieck made on Charles Follen because of the great influence exerted by Follen on important American contemporaries such as John Quincy Adams and Margaret Fuller.

Among the first Americans who had contact with Tieck are several "Göttingen men:" Bancroft, Henry Edwin Dwight, and George Ticknor. American acquaintance with German literature around 1800, even if defective, was more extensive than past critical opinion would allow, and it had been prepared by a long, slow-growing, indigenous American development of some two hundred years. It was the New Englanders who studied at Göttingen, particularly Ticknor, Edward Everett, and Bancroft, who made the introduction of German learning to America an accomplished fact. As Spindler points out:

> It was a most interesting fact that these pioneers of the new movement not only brought back with them an increased amount of knowledge and a new conception of culture and scholarship, but also the greatest enthusiasm for German educational ideas, which they now were eager to transplant upon American soil. This is shown by Ticknor's introduction of radical reforms at Harvard, of which Thomas W. Higginson could truly say: 'They laid the foundation for non-English training not only in Boston, but in America,' by taking the whole American educational system away from the English traditions and substituting the German methods. Similar influences are to be seen in Edward Everett's address on the 'Objects of a University Education,' and in Bancroft's founding of the Round Hill School after the model of the German Gymnasium.

The first contacts are those between Bancroft and Tieck. George Bancroft (1800-1891) had studied at Göttingen from 1818 to 1819. While there, he had had occasion to take Friedrich Bouterwek's course in the history of German Literature. His notes are still preserved in the Manuscript Division of the New York Public Library. Among these there is one reference to Tieck worth quoting:

> Lyric. Dahin gehören Die Minnelieder. Herausgegeben von Bothmer. Es fehlt uns eine zweckmässige Auswahl u. Bearbeitung. Benecke's Ergänzungen. Herr Tieck hat einige dieser recht hübsch bearbeitet. Aber aus den Umarbeitungen dieser Vorscher kann man nicht die Naiveté fühlen. Ein grosser Teil ist Nachahmung Provencalischer Lieder. Sie ahmen dem Ton nach. aber die Deutsche Gesinnungs-Art (?) wurde hineingetragen. Unverkennbar sind Wahrheit und Anmuth des Gefühls. Das Schwärmerische ist darinn. Auch ist es geschwätzig. Sie kommen immer auf dieselben Gedanken zurück. Strenge Richtigkeit des Ausdruckes muss man auch nicht suchen. Die Poesie entstand zu geschwind. Die Verskunst dieser Gedichte ist zu bewundern. Die Verse sind zum Theil sehr regelmässig: jedoch kommt hinzu oder fehlt sehr oft im Fuss. Eine Annäherung zum Sonnett fühlt man—jedoch kein eigentliches Sonnett. Vieles ist hier noch aufzuklären. Viele Fürsten haben sich ausgezeichnet. Merkwürdig sind einige wie Heinrich von Feldegger.

Thus, as early as 1819 at least one of Tieck's works, *Minnelieder aus dem schwäbischen Zeitalter*, 1803, was known to Bancroft.

A later reference to Tieck occurs in connection with a visit to Schulpforta, where Bancroft spent four days seeing young Frederic Henry Hedge, whom he had placed there. After a visit to its "excellent library" on March 5, 1821, Bancroft notes in his journal:

> I looked at some books; at Tieck's translation of Don Quixote, which is praised as eminently good. Tieck certainly has a lively imagination, though in his original pieces he is often tedious by the length of his descriptions.

Two days later, when Bancroft visited Goethe on March 7, 1821, he had occasion to mention Tieck to Goethe, who remained silent when Tieck's name was brought up:

> I was with Goethe for a half hour today. I felt the vast difference between him and the many scholars whom I have lately seen. Goethe has the ease of a gentleman, speaks with loveliness and

energy, but does not seem to take any longer a lively interest in the affairs of the world. I tried to bring him to talk of the German poets, and mentioned Tieck, but Goethe remained silent. I mentioned the Schlegels; he observed merely that they had written many pretty things.
I ought to mention that Goethe praised Schlegel's translation of Shakespeare and spoke of the delight he had taken in a late perusal of Julius Caesar . . .

Bancroft is probably mistaken in his explanation of Goethe's silence about Tieck and his slighting attitude toward the Schlegels. It is not because Goethe no longer took "a lively interest in the affairs of the world" that he ignored them, but because he as a classicist felt hostile toward romantic authors and all that they stood for.

A later reference to Tieck occurs in Bancroft's article, "German Literature," in Volume IV of the *American Quarterly Review*. In this article, containing a discussion of Bouterwek's *Geschichte der deutschen Poesie und Beredsamkeit*, Heeren's *Andenken an deutsche Historiker aus den letzten fünfzig Jahren*, and Franz Horn's *Umrisse*, he says about Tieck:

Of Tieck we can observe, that he is an industrious and gifted adherent of the critical school of the Schlegels; eminently *romantic*. His Genoveva is the best of his poems, which aim at a general interest. Yet, in the effort to sustain poetic interest, by the simplicity of a legendary story, he has attained a kind of excellence which will be acknowledged by a literary party, rather than by the public at large. The mind that is imbued with the peculiar spirit which is willing to discover beauties in the stiff Madonnas of the early artists, and again allows itself to be lulled into a pleasing mood by the childish attractions of an artless tale, may admire. The Alamae is deficient in power and rapidity of action.
But most of Tieck's works are destined for the home market. His brightest poetical side is polemical. Whilst the Schlegels criticised, he wrote humorous and ironical dialogues, poems, and tales. He contributed essentially to the emancipation of literature from pedantic rules, though at the same time the tendency of his works, and of those of his school generally, has likewise been to produce a feeble and affected imitation of natural excellence. Apart from his original works, Tieck has made an approved translation of Don Quixote; and he is now engaged in completing A. W. Schlegel's translation of Shakespeare. To the illustration of this author, Tieck has devoted many years; and an elaborate work on the bard of Avon is expected from him.

While the article is not signed, its authorship can be determined by the fact that it was reproduced in part in Bancroft's *Literary and Historical Miscellanies,* New York, 1855, 167-205.

These remarks are accurate for *Genoveva,* but they do not do sufficient justice to Tieck's general literary achievements which, in such works as *Der blonde Eckbert* and *Der Runenberg,* are anything but polemical or humorous and yet achieve excellence. Bancroft could not have known in 1828 that Tieck never completed his Shakespeare project.

Another tribute from a Göttingen man came from Henry Edwin Dwight in his *Travels in the North of Germany, in the Years 1825 and 1826.* The eighth child of President Timothy Dwight of Yale, Dwight lived from 1797 to 1832. He spent four years (1824 to 1828) studying at the University of Göttingen, including some travel through North Germany.

Bancroft's derogatory attitude toward Tieck's achievements as a poet in his review of Dwight's book in *The American Quarterly Review* is unduly harsh, but Dwight undoubtedly overpraises him as a critic. Tieck was engaged on his Shakespeare project during a large part of his life, but never completed it, stopping work on it in 1815. Zeydel's description of the plan of the fourth draft as given in its ninth chapter bears out Dwight's statement of his project: "He conceived three gigantic sections, each of which might have comprised several volumes and would have amounted to a general history of western Europe, as well as a history of comparative literature from about 1300 to Shakespeare's death." So also does one of the two introductory chapters of the fifth and last draft of *Das Buch über Shakespeare* (1815), which "regards Shakespeare as marking the consummation and turning point of poesy in its historical development." If by the term "poetry" Dwight meant writing in general, Tieck had certainly published a number of volumes as early as 1799. It is doubtful that Tieck ever was "the reader to the queen of Saxony," as Dwight says. It is certain that in 1824 Tieck became the "Dramaturg" of the Dresden theater, *not* its director. That post was held by Wolf Adolf von Lüttichau. Zeydel points out that Tieck's readings, especially during his Dresden period, were one of the glories of that city during the period from 1820 to 1840. They have received high praise not only from countless Germans, but from Englishmen and Americans as well. Dwight's vivid account of such a reading bears witness to Tieck's histrionic skill and confirms the general charm and attractiveness of his personality. This account also shows that not only American scholars of the highest calibre, but cultivated Americans in general, were attracted to Tieck during his Dresden period. The section on Tieck belongs to Letter XX, which is dated, "Dresden, August, 1826." This is Dwight's description of Tieck's dramatic readings, particularly his reading of *Much Ado about Nothing*:

> Tieck, at the present time, fills the office of *reader* to the queen of Saxony. He is reputed to be the best reader in Germany; no one, not even the most distinguished players, being able to modulate their voices with the same taste, and express every passion of dramatic poetry with the same eloquence as himself. To gratify his friends and others, he often reads Shakespeare to small circles assembled at his house to listen to him. I was so fortunate as to be present when he read "Much Ado about Nothing." He merely mentioned the names of the characters at the commencement of the different scenes, adapting his voice to each with an accuracy that left you never in doubt as to the *dramatis personae* who were speaking. His voice has great compass, an easy modulation, and a power which it is difficult to rival, even on the stage. The characters of the play became, under his enthusiastic elocution, real beings, and so animated were his gestures, and so marked was his face with the ever-varying expression of the characters, that it was no difficult thing to believe that you were listening to a theatrical representation. Had he embraced the profession of a player, I am convinced that he would have risen far superior to any one now living in Germany. Several of the distinguished performers on the stages of Dresden and Vienna were present at this perusal, to which they listened with the greatest interest, and with the strongest marks of approbation.

The most significant personal contact of an American "Göttingen man" with Tieck was that of George Ticknor. As this has been fully and adequately investigated by Zeydel, it is not necessary for us to do more than review it here. Ticknor (1791-1871), later a well-known Hispanist and Harvard professor, had studied at Göttingen from 1815 to 1817. He met Tieck in Dresden during his second voyage to Europe in November 1835, attracted to the German author because of his great literary reputation throughout Europe at the time. This contact deepened during the next half year to include not only Tieck but other members of his circle, such as Philalethes, Baron von Ungern-Sternberg, the young Prussian Baron Eduard von

Bülow, Frau von Lüttichau, and Raumer. One of the chief bonds between Tieck and Ticknor was their mutual interest in books and manuscripts, particularly early English drama. Ticknor had occasion to learn Tieck's theories about the pseudo-Shakespearian works, such as "Fair Emm." Tieck read a number of remarks about Goethe in Ticknor's presence, treating Goethe "with admiration indeed, but with an admiration more measured and discriminating than is usual among the Germans." Ticknor censured Goethe for his vanity, which, he said, stemmed from the constant adulation the German nation had showered upon him and which was obvious from the care with which he preserved even his most insignificant papers. Ticknor admired Tieck's brilliant readings of such plays as *Henry IV, A Midsummer-Night's Dream, As You Like It,* and *Twelfth Night.* On two occasions, Ticknor heard Tieck read a number of cantos from the translation by Prince John of Saxony of Dante's *Purgatorio* at the Prince's home, in the company of the Dresden Dante circle. The readings were followed by critical comments from the invited guests. The Ticknors stayed in Dresden until May 12, 1836. On a return trip from Berlin to Vienna on May 31, Ticknor again visited Tieck and had an opportunity to meet his younger brother, the sculptor Friedrich.

A later contact, after Ticknor's return to America in 1838, was through Francis Lieber (1800-1872), the German-American political economist. Lieber visited Germany in 1844, bringing a letter of introduction from Ticknor which Tieck acknowledged in a letter to Ticknor dated October, 1844, and found by Zeydel in Berlin. Ticknor made an effort to reach Tieck through Dr. N. H. Julius of Hamburg (who was to become the German translator of his *History of Spanish Literature*), with a view to acquiring his small but very valuable collection of Spanish books. Nothing seems to have come of this effort.

In 1849, there appeared Ticknor's *History of Spanish Literature.* He sent a copy to Tieck, who acknowledged its receipt in a letter written in Potsdam on July 28, 1850. The original of this letter seems to be lost. Only Ticknor's English translation of it in his *Life* is extant. Tieck expresses his profound admiration for Ticknor's *History,* from which he gained "an endless amount of new information." He liked particularly well the chapters on the Romances, and while he admired the religious mythical poetry as represented by Lope and Mira de Mesqua, he censured recent caricatures and modern poetry with its "modern ideas," "French style," and "degraded language."

Ticknor's *History of Spanish Literature* contains four references to Tieck. These include an acknowledgment in the preface for permission to consult his private library while Ticknor was in Germany. Ticknor praises his "very spirited, but somewhat free" translation of *El Escudero Marcos de Obregón*. He regards his translation of *Don Quixote* as superior to any other translation in German or other foreign languages, adding that it has superseded all other German versions.

Zeydel has summed up the relations between Tieck and Ticknor:

> Ticknor undoubtedly stood closer to Tieck than any other American; his relation to him was probably more intimate than to any German man of letters. They had various common interests, *viz.* their passion for books in general and for Hispanica in particular; their interest in early English and Spanish literatures, Ticknor's from the point of view of the scholar and literary historian and Tieck's from that of the Romantic poet and critic; their interest in the drama and in dramatic readings, especially of Shakespeare's plays; their study of Dante; and finally their critical, uneffusive attitude toward Goethe.

Following E. P. Whipple's statement in his *Recollections of Eminent Men*, Zeydel points out that while "possessing a better 'external knowledge' of Spanish literature than either A. W. Schlegel or Tieck ... Ticknor lacked 'imaginative sympathy and insight' and was inferior to them in the power to reproduce the spirit of a literary age." Zeydel agrees that Tieck's "attitude toward literature always remained that of a poet."

Another important scholar who came in contact with Tieck was John Lothrop Motley, the author of the *Rise of the Dutch Republic* (1856). During the course of his studies in Germany (1832 to 1835), he stayed in Berlin for a while, from 1833 to the spring of 1834. He visited Weimar, where he received a letter of introduction from Ottilie Goethe to Countess Finkenstein. He then went to Dresden, using this letter to make the acquaintance of Tieck. Afterwards he wrote to his mother about this visit, recounting his opinion of those of Tieck's writings with which he was familiar. This account may be quoted in full:

Vienna,
June 2nd, 1834.

My dear Mother,—
* * * * * * *

Madame de Goethe, of whom I spoke in my last letter, gave me a letter to a Countess Finkenstein of Dresden, an old lady who lives in Tieck's family, and by whom I was introduced to this author. I had been very much disappointed, as you know, in not having been in Germany before Goethe's death, that I might have seen that Nestor of literature, and this has been in some sort a compensation. I do not know if many of Tieck's works have been translated into English. If they have, you will get them in the Athenaeum. Inquire for 'Fantasas' or 'Puss in Boots' or the 'World upside down,' or Tieck's novels (which last are a set of exquisite little tales, novels in the original meaning of the word), full of old German legends and superstitions, and the authorship of which will entitle him to the title of German 'Boccaccio.' The other works are the old nursery tales of 'Fortunatus,' 'Puss in Boots,' 'Blue Beard,' etc., etc., done into plays (not for the stage), and as full of playful and sharp satire, poetry and plain sense as they can hold. If they have not been translated we shall have a chance of reading them together one of these days. I was invited by Tieck to tea on Sunday evening, when there was a small party. He is at present just about finishing his translation of Shakespeare (in company with Schlegel), and is in the habit of reading a play aloud to a party of select auditors. I did not hear him, and rather regret it, because he seems to be rather vain of his elocution. His head and bust are fine, and it was not till he got up from his chair that I observed he was slightly deformed (humpbacked). His conversation was like his books, playful, full of *bonhomie*, good natured sort of satire, and perhaps a little childish vanity. He spoke of Cooper, Irving (whom he knew in Dresden, and whom he admired very much), steamboats, homoeopathism, himself, elocution, wit, Shakespeare and the musical glasses. His conversation was pleasing and quiet, but without any great show or brilliancy; "and so much for Buckingham."

Bancroft's attitude toward Goethe and Tieck is quite different from that of Motley. This difference expresses the change in attitude between the previous and the contemporary generations. Motley's interest in Tieck persisted, for he translated Tieck's drama *The Blue Beard* in *The New World* in 1840.

Edward Robinson (1794-1863), professor of theology at Andover, and later at Union Theological Seminary, travelled from 1826 to 1830 in Europe and met Tieck during this period.

Hugh Swinton Legaré (1797-1843), the renowned lawyer and statesman who was *chargé d'affaires* at Brussels from 1832 to

1833, attempted to meet Tieck while he was taking a trip through Germany in 1836. Legaré was a personal friend of Ticknor's. He had met him in Dresden around the first of May and had spent a good part of his five-day visit there in his company. In a journal in which he recorded his travel experiences down the Rhine and through Germany, Legaré makes the following notation under the date, "Munich, 11th May. (1836) :"

> Ticknor proposed I should hear Tieck read a play of Shakespeare. He is, you know, the renowned *collaborateur* of Schlegel in his translation, and is famous as a reader; but once he begins he must go thro'. This rather alarmed me, yet I consented, but unfortunately he was ill.

Francis Lieber acted as Ticknor's intermediary on one of his visits to Berlin in 1844. He visited Berlin in July and again in October, 1844, on a return trip to that city, and brought a letter from Ticknor to Tieck, dated Boston, March 5, 1844, in which Ticknor recommends him "as a man of talent and great knowledge, of a faithful and excellent character." Tieck apparently answered this letter. A draft of it was discovered by Zeydel in Berlin and published in his article on "Tieck and Ticknor." It is not mentioned in Ticknor's diary, nor is there any trace of an original among the Ticknor papers. Yet it is not unreasonable to assume that the letter was sent. In this letter, which is dated "im Oktober 1844," Francis Lieber is mentioned twice. He is referred to at the beginning:

> Wie sehr Sie mich erfreut haben mit dem Blatte, das ich aus der Hand des ausgezeichneten und liebenswürdigen Amerikaners Francis Lieber empfing, kann ich Ihnen kaum sagen.

Later Tieck says:

> In Ihrem prächtigen Hn. Francis Lieber habe ich einen Mann von grossem Talent kennen gelernt—einen engeren Landsmann von mir, in Berlin geboren, wie ich von ihm selber erfuhr. Preussen hat in ihm einen tüchtigen Menschen verloren, Amerika einen feinsinnigen Gelehrten gewonnen.

Both of these statements, brief as they are, show the high opinion that Tieck had of Lieber. In 1832 an article on Tieck appeared in the *Encyclopaedia Americana,* of which Lieber at that time was editor-in-chief. This, like the whole encyclopaedia, was based on the seventh edition of the German (Brockhaus) Conversations-Lexicon. That Tieck was considered of sufficient importance to continue to be included in the *Encyclopaedia Americana* may be seen by the fact that an article on him was published in the 1941 edition and reprinted in the 1947 edition.

Zeydel also mentions a meeting between Tieck and an American named Walter Haven. Unfortunately, beyond the source in Holtei, which merely mentions his name, no further information about him can be found.

The meetings of Tieck with Irving and Cooper, also mentioned by Zeydel, and the meeting with Motley will be discussed in the chapter on American authors.

Overshadowing the influence of such native American scholars as Ticknor and Bancroft is the great germinal influence of Charles Follen. Through the efforts of Ticknor and Mr. Du Ponceau, Dr. Follen was appointed teacher of the German language in Harvard College in 1825. He was promoted to a professorship in 1830, holding this post until 1835. His influence in stimulating an interest in German language and literature and, incidentally, in Tieck was very strong. He compiled one of the earliest and most influential German readers and grammars in the country and contributed considerably to the rise of interest in German literature in Cambridge and Boston. He was a very popular and effective teacher. In a letter of August 24, 1829, he notes:

> The study of the German language and literature is steadily increasing. Many young Americans, particularly theological students, who have finished their studies here, are traveling to Germany, in order to begin there anew, and then to make the dead riches of German learning live here anew in this free air.

In his Inaugural Address in 1831, on the occasion of his appointment to his professorship, he was able to say:

> In this our own country, and particularly in this literary vicinity, the attention which is paid to this portion of universal literature, is within the observation of all who hear me. The treasures contained in German works did not escape public notice, but soon gained the intelligent interest which is taken here in everything that promises to enlarge and elevate the mind. In this university, where formerly German lore was classed under the head of "non leguntur," the library has lately been augmented by a considerable number of valuable works; German books, in their native type, are issuing from the University press; and there is every year an average number of fifty students of the German language. There are German books and teachers in every place

of importance in this country. In Boston, particularly, where, as I am assured, about fifty years ago, not a German grammar or dictionary was to be found, there are now a number of persons who speak, and a large number who read, and enter into the sense and spirit of German works. Many German authors have already found a place in private libraries, among the literary representatives of other countries, and gladden the eye of the stranger whose heart is not yet weaned from the pleasures of his childhood, the guides of his youth, and the great standards of his manhood.

Follen's inaugural address elicited a very enthusiastic and interesting reply from John Quincy Adams, and Follen must have inspired Margaret Fuller and other important personages in whose circles he moved at Cambridge and Boston to deepen their study of German.

Follen's great influence as a teacher of German literature contributed to a favorable interest in Tieck. Follen himself was evidently an admirer of the German poet. He included large selections from Tieck in his reader. In the first edition of his *Deutsches Lesebuch für Anfänger* in 1826, Follen included from Tieck *Der Blonde Eckbert* and the poem "Die Lilie Romanze." His later editions, beginning with the second of 1831, contained selections from *Blaubart* and *Der gestiefelte Kater*, as well as the poems "Frühling" and "Der Verschmähte." The posthumous G. A. Schmitt edition of 1858 contained no prose and only the poems "Frühling" and "Der Verschmähte." In his inaugural address Follen lists the name of Tieck with those who contributed most to the glory of modern German literature:

> Of those illustrious men to whom this new republic of letters owes its existence and its glory, I mention only the names of Lessing, Klopstock, Wieland, Herder, Goethe, Schiller, Richter, and Tieck. It would be doing injustice to these worthies to take so brief a notice of their literary character, as the nature of this occasion would require;—even if their merits were not too generally known to render it necessary.

In his reply to an inquiry from John Quincy Adams concerning the merits of Richter and Tieck, Follen, after dealing with Richter at some length, says:

> Tieck stands at the head of the romantic school in Germany. His most interesting productions are contained in a collection of tales and plays, called 'Phantasus.' There is no writer that I know, who has called forth and unfolded more powerfully that principle

in our nature, which makes us capable alike of true religion and of superstition; a principle which is, perhaps, of all the most characteristic feature in the German character; that simplicity, which walks by faith, which is ever ready to believe what it has not seen; and, though it receives many things without reason, has, on the other hand, the privilege of perceiving what reason cannot see; what is hidden from the wise and the prudent, and revealed to the simple. The tales of Tieck are characterized by a continuous transition from the most simple everyday events of life, to those which lie beyond all experience and all calculation. This intimate connexion at once gives to the miraculous the assurance of experience, and to the simplest reachings of the heart their true heavenly import, by showing that credulity is but the infancy of faith.

While Tieck was among the first, who directed the misguided taste of the public to the true sources of sentiment and poetry, he wrote the death-warrant of a sickly sentimentality in his 'Puss in Boots' (Der gestiefelte Kater), the best, if not the only good German comedy; making the stage an Aristophanic self-exhibition of authors and critics, the public and the court.

CHAPTER TWO

TIECK'S RECEPTION IN AMERICAN MAGAZINES AND BOOKS PRIOR TO 1900

A.

Tieck's Reception in American Magazines Prior to 1900

Tieck's popularity in American magazines is a good index of his general popularity. Contrary to the general trends for German literature pointed out by Goodnight and Haertel, the first reference to Tieck in an American journal is a short five-line item in the *American Monthly Magazine and Critical Review*, 1818, and not until 1825 does the steady flow of references begin. 1836 and 1844 are 'peak years,' with three and four items occurring in each. The death of Tieck evokes three items. The number begins to taper off markedly after 1856, there being only four items in 1868, 1875, 1881, and 1888, except for the articles by Boyesen in 1875 and 1876 and a short note by Kuno Francke in 1895. The latter items are part of the scholarly interest in Tieck which comes to its full flower in the twentieth century. Therefore, instead of the two periods from 1817 to 1832, and from 1833 to 1845 which, according to Goodnight, mark the inception and the culmination of real interest in German literature, we may speak of one large span beginning about the middle of the first interval, 1825, and continuing past the *terminus ad quem* of the second one, 1856. Haertel gives support to this view when he states that the earlier years covered by his investigation, 1846 to 1880, were marked by an interest in individual members of the Romantic School, but as with Tieck, disappeared almost entirely before the close of this period.

The first magazine item is noteworthy only for showing the beginning of interest in Tieck by American magazines. It occurs in *The American Monthly Magazine and Critical Review*, IV, 1818, 142, and advertises the appearance of the first two volumes of Tieck's *German Theatre*.

The item for 1825 in *The Museum of Foreign Literature and Science*, VII, 1825, 270, is a notice of *The German Novelists*, which is described as "a series of Tales, Romances and Novels," with selections from the works of Tieck among others. This work is advertised anonymously as being "by the Translator of Wilhelm Meister and Author of the Life of Schiller. 3 vols."

It must, therefore, be an advance reference to Carlyle's *German Romance*, which appeared in 1827.

The item in *The New-York Literary Gazette and Phi Beta Kappa Repository*, I, September, 1825, to March, 1826, is more significant. It contains the first American translation of a work by Tieck, *Liebeszauber*, under the title, *The Love Charm. A Tale from the German of Tieck*. The issue for January 21, 1826, 305-306, contains the first review of Ludwig Tieck in any American magazine and demonstrates by its warm praise and understanding of Tieck the trend at this time toward a better appreciation of German literature, particularly of German romanticism. "There is not in the whole history of literature," the reviewer states, "any poet who can count up so many and so great exploits achieved in his first descent into the arena; in number and variety even Goethe must yield the precedence, though his youthful triumphs were *Goetz von Berlichingen* and *Werther*." He then proceeds to praise in Tieck's early works "the promise, and far more than the promise, of the greatest dramatic poet whom Europe had seen since the days of Calderón." He characterizes his humor as "the living merriment," "the incarnation, so to say, of the principle of mirth in Shakespeare, and Cervantes, and Aristophanes." He cites "as a wreath of flowers to crown the whole . . . the heavenly purity and starlike loveliness of his *Genoveva* . . . Had the rest of Tieck's life kept pace with the fertility of the six years from 1798 to 1804 he must have been beyond all rivalry the second of German poets; and as Eschylus in *The Frogs* shares his supremacy with Sophocles, so would Goethe have invited Tieck to sit beside him on the throne." The reviewer then deals with Tieck's collection of tales and later dramas, briefly mentions his later novellistic period—rare among American critics of Tieck—and pays special tribute to his proposed "great work upon Shakespeare." He mentions what he considers Tieck's exceptional qualifications for it, including his uniting "in such perfection of the great critic with the great poet" and concludes: "One may look forward therefore with confidence to the greatest work in aesthetical criticism that even Germany will ever have produced." This grandiose project, which Tieck had planned and begun in his student days and thought about almost to the end of his life, was never completed. It was to describe the entire course of modern poetry, of which the cardinal point in Tieck's opinion was Shakespeare. This evaluation of Shakespeare might have been an epoch-making contribution, more so for its poetic intuitions than its scholarly achievements, since Tieck ignored the findings of English Shakespearean scholars.

The next item shows the close link between British and American criticism in this period. It appears in *The Museum of Foreign Literature and Science* for April, 1827, X, 289-297, merely as a reprint from *The (London) Monthly Review*. It seems to have escaped Zeydel's notice in his *Tieck and England*. It deals with "Tieck's Dramatic Criticisms" and discusses performances at the Dresden theater as well as those which Tieck observed during his trip to England and during his theatrical tour through Germany when he emphasized Shakespearean roles and characters.

A reprint in the *Museum of Foreign Literature and Science*, XVII, July to December, 1830, 283-5, from the *New Monthly Magazine*, entitled "Specimens of German Genius," is dealt with in the chapter on translations.

An item not mentioned by Goodnight appears in *The Foreign Quarterly Review*, No. 22, and is reprinted in *The Select Journal of Foreign Periodical Literature*, No. IV, October, 1833, 209-10. The article is in the form of a review and is entitled, "Art. IV.—Briefe aus Paris, zur Erläuterung der Geschichte des sechzehnten und siebzehnten Jahrhunderts. Von Friedrich von Raumer," (with an English sub-title) and is dated, "Leipzig, 1831." The reviewer states that "the letters are addressed to the celebrated Ludwig Tieck." A part of the first of these is quoted. Here Raumer explains that he uses the letter form because of "the detached and isolated" nature of the subject matter. Since Tieck possesses such an accurate knowledge of history, he will be able "to understand and arrange everything in its proper connexion with what is already known." The dedication, he adds, offers further "proof of an old and faithful friendship—although none such be needed!"

In a review of Carlyle's *Life of Friedrich Schiller* in *The Christian Examiner and General Review*, Boston, 1834, XVI, written by Frederic Henry Hedge, we find two brief references to Tieck. In the first Hedge seeks to defend the Germans against the charge that they lack epic power because of their excessive interest in philosophy, although later he criticizes them for a general tendency to too great expansiveness in epic composition.

> This feature in German works of fiction [their interest in philosophy] proceeds rather from a peculiarity of taste, than from want of epic power, the existence of which, in that nation, has been sufficiently proved by many of their lighter works, particularly by those of Tieck, Hoffmann, and Baron Motte Fouqué.

In a later statement Tieck, along with Schiller, is declared to be international:

> To this general rule, Schiller forms a remarkable exception. There never was a poet in whose works unity and wholeness, harmony of form and concentration of interest, were more conspicuous than in his. In this respect he seems less intimately related to his own country than most of his contemporaries. We cannot subscribe to the sentence which has pronounced him a peculiarly *national* poet. We know of no German writer, unless it be Tieck, who is less German.

A review which appeared originally in *Blackwood's Edinburgh Magazine* entitled "Shakespeare in Germany" and reprinted in *The Museum of Foreign Literature and Science*, XXVI, 1835, 554ff., criticizes opinions held by Tieck on Hamlet, Claudius, Polonius and Ophelia, but praises Tieck's insight into the technique of stage representation. Since this is a reprint from an English journal, it is discussed in Zeydel's *Tieck and England*.

In 1836, there were numerous articles which referred to Tieck. He is mentioned in George Calvert's lecture on German literature, reprinted from *The Southern Literary Messenger*, Baltimore, 1836, which praises German literature and culture in general most highly.

In an article entitled "Present State of Germany," which appeared in *The American Monthly Magazine*, July, 1836, there is a review of Haven's translation of Heine's *Letters auxiliary to the History of Modern Polite Literature in Germany*. The reviewer reserves for later numbers a detailed examination of such authors mentioned by Heine as Arnim, Hoffmann, Novalis, Lessing, Herder, and Tieck. While he agrees with Heine's remarks, he takes exception to the severity of his censure upon Tieck's "first manner." "William Lovell," he states, "though not what is called a well-written book, is full of genius" and displays two qualities in Tieck quoted from Heine's impressions of that author. The first is his blending of the lyrist and satirist. The second is Heine's marvellous description of the spirit of Tieck's Novellen *Der blonde Eckbert* and *Der Runenberg,* their peculiar identification of man with nature, and the mysterious, medieval charm of Tieck's imagination, which Heine likens to a chaste yet yearning noble lady.

Another review of this translation, written by C. Beck, appeared in *The North American Review,* XLIII, Boston, 1836, 166, 169-70, 176-78. The reviewer cites as an example of Heine's poetical talent, "his description of the muse of Tieck." He quotes Heine's condemnation of Tieck's romantic muse as infantile and later in the review develops his views of Heine's poetical talent in considerable detail. The reviewer regards Tieck as "one of the more distinguished, perhaps the most distinguished of the Romantic School." After Schlegel Heine submits Tieck to "a close scrutiny, the result of which, though by no means indicating a friendly spirit, is upon the whole correct, and acknowledges his unquestionable genius." The three "manners" which Heine observes in Tieck, the rationalistic, the romantic, and the realistic, are considered in some detail, and a fine excerpt is quoted from Haven's translation, in which Heine characterizes Tieck's second period. The reviewer's concluding remarks on Heine's characterization of Tieck defend Heine's criticism of Tieck's three manners as being "a strange discrepancy between the understanding and the imagination." They appear to him as "the principal stages of a perfectly natural and spontaneous process of the inner man."

In an article entitled, "Thomas Carlyle The German Scholar" of the February, 1838, issue of *The Western Messenger,* VI, 422-423, Carlyle is credited with having "nearly broken down the wall of division which rose between the two great and kindred literatures of England and Germany" by "his excellent translations, as well as by his spirited articles in various periodicals." He comments on the growth of German literature since Carlyle had begun to write eight or ten years before, as attested by the maturer work of Goethe and Schiller and such authors as "Richter, Novalis, Tieck, and a whole crowd of master-spirits," who had "carved out for themselves a home in the intellectual community." He concludes: "Much praise then, to Mr. Carlyle, for having introduced us to this fair circle of gifted minds."

Other pertinent articles in *The North American Review* (1843, LVII, 433-458), include a review of Steffens' autobiography, *Was ich erlebte*, which appeared in Breslau from 1840 to 1842. The reviewer, relying heavily on this work, takes up the life and significance of Steffens and shows in the course of his discussion certain points of contact between Steffens and Tieck. He notes that Steffens was a friend and contemporary of "the famous Jena circle," including such figures as Goethe, Schiller, Fichte, Schelling, Tieck, Novalis, and the Schlegels. In Jena, Tieck drew a caricature of Steffens and Friedrich Schlegel. On a visit to Dresden, Steffens met Tieck. At this point the reviewer quotes a translation of an interesting description of Tieck, and Steffens' warm and fruitful relations with Tieck are summarized:

> The benefit I have derived from intercourse with him (Tieck) during the progress of a friendship of the most intimate character and of very long duration, even though we have differed on subjects of the highest moment, is greater than I can express.

Passing mention of Tieck also occurs in a review of Gervinus' *History of German Poetry* in *The North American Review*, 1844, LVIII, 108. The reviewer refers to Tieck as "the humorous and romantic reproducer of the fable of the Middle Ages."

Mrs. Ellet's article on "German Novelists," which appeared in *The Ladies' Companion*, June, 1840, XIII, 87-9, deals chiefly with Tieck's *Novellen*. It praises Tieck for his services in correcting the aberrations of his countrymen through his reasonableness and his morality, and it lauds the excellence of his style. There are brief discussions of the *Wundersuchtigen (sic), Des Dichters Leben (sic), Der Hexen Sabbath (sic), Das Zauberschloss, Die Verlobung, Der Yahrmarkt (sic)*, and *Pietro von Albano*. Mrs. Ellet dwells at greater length on *Musikalische Leiden und Freuden*, and *Die Riesenden (sic)*, from each of which she translates a passage, despite her own stricture of those *Novellen* which "have little interest for foreign readers, as the lash of satire is there applied to the follies and vices of German provincial life." In her conclusions she cites the lack of excitement and the calmness with which Tieck generally proceeds in his tales. She praises once more his sober reasonableness which has as its object to correct "a prevailing vice in letters." She ends by lauding his productions as being "calculated to work good that shall endure when the most extravagant flights of imagination have ceased to astonish."

We now come to the all-important *Dial*. Although the references to Tieck are cursory and scattered, they are made by outstanding persons. In Volume I of *The Dial* Theodore Parker, in his epoch-making article on "German Literature" (January, 1841, 315-39), comments on the general originality of the staple of German literature and adds the following:

> In point of freshness, it has no equal since the days of Sophocles. Who shall match with Wieland, and Lessing, the Schlegels, Herder, so sweet and beautiful, Jean-Paul, Tieck, and Schiller, and Goethe? We need not mention lesser names, nor add more of their equals.

There are two brief references to an apoplectic stroke suffered by Tieck in the summer of 1842, one more optimistic than the other. They appear in Volume III in the section headed "Literary Intelligence" under the dates "Heidelberg, Oct. 20, 1842" and "Heidelberg, Jan. 5, 1843," and were probably written by Charles Stearns Wheeler.

There are also several incidental references to Tieck in connection with other matters. In a review of a *Life of Jean Paul Richter*, 1842, the following comment is made, under date of January, 1843, about the style of German writers in general:

> The Germans are more given to speculate than to narrate. Their very novels, Lafontaine's, Lamotte-Fouqué's, Jean Paul's, Tieck's, are not so much stories as they are theories of life.

Another reference appears in an article by Emerson in volume IV, titled "A Letter" (October, 1843):

> But passing to a letter which is a generous and just tribute to Bettina von Arnim, we have it in our power to furnish our correspondent and all sympathizing readers with a sketch, though plainly from no friendly hand, of the new work of that eminent lady, who in the silence of Tieck and Schelling, seems to hold a monopoly of genius in Germany.

Margaret Fuller, in her article in *The Dial* on "The Modern Drama" on the occasion of her vindication of the actor's profession, points out the greater respect accorded the profession in Germany, as seen in the sketches by Tieck of that country's great actors:

> In Germany these questions have already been fairly weighed, and those who read the sketches of her great actors, as given by

Tieck, know that there, at least, they took with the best minds of their age and country their proper place.

A critical notice of a work entitled, *Puss in Boots and the Marquis of Carabas. A pure translation from the original German*, New York, 1844, appeared in the *Columbian Magazine*, New York, 1844, II, 192. This is not a translation at all but a work by Mrs. Osgood for which she presumably got the idea from Tieck. Goodnight is wrong in ascribing this item to Tieck. "Mrs. Osgood," states the author of this article, "a writer of considerable reputation in our country, has recently published a new Puss in Boots ... We have been so much pleased with Mrs. Osgood's performance, that we have been tempted to turn from it to that capital comedy, the Gestiefelle Kater (*sic*) of Ludwig Tieck, from which Mrs. Osgood, we presume, borrowed the idea of her work...."

More important is the estimate of Tieck which appeared in Article VI of *The Southern Quarterly Review* for October, 1844, VI, 428-45. The writer points out that contemporary German literature in the field of prose fiction is poorer than that of Spain and Italy. It seems singular to him that this should apply to "so imaginative and reflecting a people as the Germans, possessing a literature that surpasses in fertility and elevation that of almost any other European nation." In discussing contemporary German prose writers, including such figures as Zschokke, Spindler, Tromlitz, Hoffmann, Hauff, and the Countess Hahn-Hahn, he cites Ludwig Tieck as standing at the head of the German novelists. The review contains several slight errors, such as dating the beginning of *Lovell* 1792 instead of 1793, misnaming *Dichterleben* as *Des Dichters Leben*, misspelling *Die Wundersüchtigen* as *Die Wundersuchtigen*, *Der Jahrmarkt* as *Der Yahrmarkt*, and *Der Aufruhr in den Cevennen* as *Der Aufruhr in den Sevennen*, but on the whole, it is accurate and just. It may be questioned whether *Dichterleben* is the best of Tieck's Novellen. This depends on whether one inclines more to his romantic or his historical genre. A large number of works, including *Abdallah* and *Lovell, Pietro von Abano*, the *Zauberschloss*, and *Vittoria Accarombona* (*sic*), are discussed briefly and accurately. The review shows the rare quality in the literary criticism of the time of giving proper emphasis to Tieck's later as well as his earlier novellistic period. Its judgment of Tieck tends to over-emphasize his melancholy, but it does justice to two of his abiding qualities: his moral earnestness and his subjectivity.

In Erich P. Hofacker's study, *German Literature as Reflected in the German-Language Press of St. Louis Prior to 1898*, St. Louis, 1946, there are included only a few scattered references to Tieck. By 1835, when the first German-language weekly was published in St. Louis, "Romanticism as a literary movement was approaching the end of its course. The age of realism was about to be ushered in, to hold its sway until the close of the century. A revival of interest in Romanticism does not become apparent until we reach the threshold of the new century. It is not surprising then that prior to 1900 we find only a few scattered references to the German Romanticists." In this respect the reaction of the St. Louis press to romanticism and Tieck differs from that of the Atlantic seaboard magazines. The two references to Tieck are reprints in 1845 by the *Deutsche Tribüne* of two of Tieck's shorter stories, *Die Klausenburg*, May 2-29, 1845, and *Das Zauberschloss*, November 13—December 4, 1845. Hofacker states that *Die Klausenburg* ended on May 26. Actually it ended on May 29. Hofacker's remark that they were reputedly written to ridicule E. T. A. Hoffmann's ghost stories applies more to *Das Zauberschloss* than to *Die Klausenburg*, since the former is in part "a parody of E. T. A. Hoffmann's spook stories," whereas the latter "seems to rival the ghost stories of the much despised E. T. A. Hoffmann," and unlike *Das Zauberschloss*, "it is not written in a burlesque vein." These two stories may be regarded as contemporary literature since Tieck was still alive when his stories were printed in this newspaper.

An article on Tieck's *Gestiefelter Kater*, signed 'L', in *The Southern Quarterly Review*, Charleston, 1846, IX, 237-43, deserves special comment because of the unusual fullness of the treatment and the charm of the style. Taking as his point of departure a recent illustrated publication by Mrs. Osgood of "a new Puss in Boots," he expresses his pleasure with her performance and turns from it to a consideration of "that capital comedy, the Gestiefelle Kater (*sic*) of Ludwig Tieck." (It is regrettable that this error persistently recurs whenever the play is mentioned in the article, a blemish in an otherwise deserving review.) From an age whose taste, he fears, is degenerating, he turns nostalgically to the past. He lauds the "ever living freshness and beauty" in the best German writers of the past generation and expresses his admiration for Ludwig Tieck, the rival of the celebrated Göthe (*sic*), because of his greatness as a critic and scholar. He points out how long it took for Tieck's work to be recognized, but cites its general acceptance now as an indication that it is "among the first of the poet's dramatic works . . . Many of its scenes are replete with keen wit and satire, and most unsparingly does the author apply the lash to reigning, arbitrary error." Much as he might have enjoyed the composition of this early effort, in which he gave free wing to his fancy, Tieck could never have anticipated its great success.

An account in a foreign journal, cited by "L," had referred to the strong effect produced by a performance of this play at Potsdam a year previously. This performance on April 20, 1844, was not produced at Tieck's suggestion, and it was but a moderate success. Yet there can be no doubt that Tieck must have thought well of his piece to venture so often to use the device of romantic irony, "where his pit performers freely vent their jests on the play itself." This device was used by Aristophanes and Shakespeare, and was, as Tieck says in the preface, taken from Holberg, Ben Jonson, and Fletcher.

The reviewer then translates a number of passages from the play as illustrations of the keenness of Tieck's wit and satire. These include the puss's condemnation of his master's eagerness for a quick and favorable turn of fortune, a counsel which "must have been rather superfluous to the prudent Mynheers of Tieck's time, but might well suit the eagerness for acquisition which characterizes the people of our land." There is also a translation of the dinner scene, with its irresistibly ludicrous comic pathos when the king discovers that his rabbit has been burned by the cook. The reviewer criticizes the weakness of the concluding action of the piece, when compared with "the stirring machinery of the foregoing scenes," as being at best "humorous" rather than "dramatic," and considers that it "casts a shadow on that discriminating taste, which otherwise so well conceived and executed its part." He concludes with the hope that his sampling of the play "may serve to excite the further curiosity of our readers."

A reprint from the *Tribune* in *Littell's Living Age,* April-June, 1850, XXV, 67, is only a brief notice. It reports the sale at auction on December 18 of Tieck's library and regrets that Tieck, "who has been so well patronized by the royal Maecenas," must see "his cherished treasures . . . sent away to every part of the world." The library was really purchased by the great book-seller Asher for "a mere song" as agent of the British Museum. The facts about the part played by the king in the sale of Tieck's library are somewhat different. After it had been auctioned by Asher late in 1849, despite the mortgage held on it by Brockhaus, the king caused over eleven thousand volumes to be repurchased and restored to Tieck. Yorck then secretly paid six thousand talers to Tieck on condition that after their owner's death the books would pass into his possession. The attitude of Frederick William IV and Tieck's noble friend Yorck was far more sympathetic than the *Tribune* reporter believed.

In 1853, the year of Tieck's death, there appeared a number of notices about the author. *Littell's Living Age,* April-June, 1853, XXXVII, 766-67, reprints a fairly long article about Tieck from the *Athenaeum.* This is the first of its kind in America to turn against romanticism in favor of a realistic attitude to literature. Since it appeared originally in an English journal, and has already been dealt with by Zeydel, we need not discuss it further here. Another brief notice about Tieck's death occurs in the June 4, 1853, issue of *The Literary World,* XII, 460. The writer or the typesetter substituted *Phantasms* for *Phantasus.* The writer also corrects the erroneous statement made in the *Athenaeum* article that Tieck's library had been dispersed by stating that, although it was advertised for sale at auction, "the purchase was made entire, if we recollect rightly, by the king of Prussia; so that the rare collection is still preserved." The August, 1853, issue of Literary Miscellanies of *The Eclectic Magazine of Foreign Literature, Science, and Art,* 1853, XXIX, 568, refers to Tieck in a brief notice as "not only the contemporary but the rival of Schiller and Goethe" whose "name is not unworthy to be linked with theirs." It also quotes a remark by Goethe on the merits of different authors: "I feel myself greater than Tieck, but I am immeasurably inferior to Shakespeare!" This quotation is derived from Goethe's statement to Eckermann on March 30, 1824, recorded in the latter's *Gespräche*. Goethe says that while he and Tieck are favorably disposed toward one another, there is a peculiar quality in Tieck's relations with him. This is due neither to himself nor to Tieck but rather to the Schlegels, who, in looking for someone to counterbalance Goethe, used Tieck for this purpose, and, in order to make him a worthy rival in the eyes of the public, overpraised his qualities. This created a difficulty in their relationship. For while Goethe recognizes his unusual merits, he considers it just as great an error to attempt to place Tieck on the same level as himself, as it would be for himself to imply equality with Shakespeare.

The Eclectic Magazine of January, 1854, XXXI, 51-65, reprints a fairly long article on Ludwig Tieck from *The British Quarterly Review*. Tieck's works, such as the *Sternbald, Genoveva, Octavianus,* and *Fortunatus,* are discussed. Part of Zerbino's "Garden of Poetry" and excerpts from the *Vittoria Accorombona* are translated. The reviewer shows the same bias against romanticism as was evidenced in the *Athenaeum* review. His conclusion too is that Tieck, in his later years, broke away from romanticism, having become increasingly aware of its many errors and extremes.

Until the second decade of the twentieth century, the gaps between the reviews become wider and their number smaller. We do not hear about Tieck again in the journals until 1868. Then there appeared in *The Southern Review,* Baltimore, 1868, III, 75-99, a review of *Die Elfen* and *Rothkäppchen* which contains a discussion of German romanticism in general. After treating Mörike and Immermann in some detail, the reviewer (identified by Haertel as C. W. Hutson) analyzes Tieck's contribution to German literature. He states that Tieck's chief fame in Germany derived from his "fine readings to select circles from the choicest writers of the past," through which he drew to Dresden for almost twenty years the lettered men of Germany, and that after his removal to Berlin he continued his readings before the Prussian court. The reviewer characterizes his literary career as "one of continuous opposition to the classical school of Goethe and Schiller, in favor of the old German art," and with even greater energy to the *Sturm und Drang* writers, whose "exaggeration of expression" and "absurdly unnatural effects" the reviewer strongly condemns. It is curious that he singles out such widely divergent writers as Luise Mühlbach (Clara Mundt) and Grillparzer, as Storm and Stress writers, possibly because he was acquainted only with Grillparzer's *Ahnfrau*. While it is true that Tieck was opposed to the classical tradition, his opposition to the Storm and Stress movement, by which he himself had been influenced in his early years, was neither so violent nor so extensive as the reviewer contends.

He then discusses Tieck's *Genoveva*, in which he rightly finds that "dramatic contour is sacrificed to lyrical grace and elegance." He claims that Tieck's "taste for the grotesque and his humour, as weird but not as fresh and simple as Fouqué's, make him far better fitted for success in the *Märchen* than in elaborate and complex narratives." As examples of his highest art, he singles out *Puss in Boots, Blue Beard, Little Red Riding Hood,* and the *Elves*. Such works as *The World Turned Topsy-turvy, Zerbino or the Tour in search of Taste, Tannenhäuser, Fair Haired Eckbert,* and the *Runenberg,* however, "all show the wild mixture of fun and pathos, of artistic faith and critical skepticism, in his double nature."

There follows a translation of the passage from *Zerbino* in which Cervantes appears in the Garden of Poesy. *Little Redcap* delights him with its mixture of innocence and sophisticated humor. Concluding with the *Elves,* he finds its "delicious beauty . . . appreciated by too many English readers to need any commendation here" and refers the reader to an English version of it which may be found in Hedge's *Prose Writers of Germany*.

By far the most scholarly treatment of the Romantic School in any of the journals appeared in three articles by Hjalmar H. Boyesen in *The Atlantic Monthly,* vols. XXXVI, XXXVII, between July, 1875, and May, 1876. The third of these, "Literary Aspects of The Romantic School," May, 1876, XXXVII, 607-16, discusses individual authors. Tieck, Boyesen writes, may be called "a Goethe in miniature," not because he was an imitator of Goethe, "but rather that he fulfilled in a different sphere a similar mission, standing in the Romantic camp as the *facile princeps,* as Goethe did among the classicists." Tieck is represented in his early period as caught between the Enlightenment and Storm and Stress. Boyesen points out the elements of horror and fatalism in Tieck which had already appeared in his immature productions and which became distinguishing traits of Romantic literature. They may be seen in his early work, *The Parting (Der Abschied)*. *Abdallah,* like *Almansur,* is rather a monument of Tieck's extraordinary precocity and industry than of his genius. Boyesen praises "the vividness of [Tieck's] colors, his analytical skill and his abundant rhetorical resources" in *William Lovell,* but he considers it lacking in "genuine vital force." He sketches Tieck's rationalistic episode with Nicolai and the *Straussfedern*. Zeydel takes exception with Boyesen's statement that the parallel novel, *Peter Leberecht*, is purely rationalistic. It should rather be regarded as transitional to his romantic period.

Tieck's interest in the *Märchen* is next discussed. Wackenroder first drew Tieck's attention to mediaeval folk poetry. This, in turn, the former derived from Erduin Julius Koch, Wackenroder's private tutor and an authority on mediaeval German literature. To this influence, however, must be added that of Shakespeare, Tieck's own reaction against rationalism, and his love of wonder and horror. The chap-books were only one of the sources on which he drew. This interest led, as Boyesen states, to "numerous dramatic and novelistic adaptations of the national legends with which he flooded the market and the stage during the next twenty years." Boyesen mentions specifically *The Life and Death of St. Genevieve,* and states that "among his many excellent tales" the critics usually give preference to *The Blonde Eckbert, Tannhäuser, The Faithful Eckart,* and *The Runenberg,* "all of which are included in the collection of Phantasies." (It seems strange that so well-informed a critic should use this appellation for *Phantasus*.)

Boyesen's analysis of the *Märchen* is particularly good. He shows how Tieck passes from the simple primitive credulity of the folk-tale proper, which he tries to reproduce in *The Children of Heymon,* to a more subjective treatment that gives vent to his own "warm and passionate life" and serves as "the vehicle of some individual sentiment, mood, or passion." This treatment is clumsy and inartistic in his *Love-Story of the Beautiful Magelone and the Count Peter of Provence,* but it reaches its height in the style of *The Runenberg* and *The Blonde Eckbert*. He quotes Heine's famous passage characterizing these *Märchen*, and shows how they contain the qualities already observed in

The Parting and *Karl von Berneck,* resulting in their excellent representation of the boundary-line between the "two realms of reason and mystery." He and his school introduced these "sepulchral situations" into literature, together with such elements as the moonlight and the interest in mediaeval history and literature. He considers Tieck's best work superior to the trend of the later Romantic School, as represented by Hoffmann and Achim von Arnim, who had reduced "the art of arousing sensations of horror to a complete system, and thereby vulgarized it." In his best work he refrains "from those violent and purely physical effects which in these latter days have made the Romantic name synonymous with literary clap-trap and charlatanism . . . and when men of Hoffmann's and Brentano's calibre had brought the school into irrevocable decay," Tieck "gradually withdrew from it, and joined the ranks of its opponents." In Tieck's lyrical work, under the influence of Wackenroder's theory, sense is made secondary to sound. Under Wackenroder's influence, Tieck, like later romanticists, developed an enthusiasm for "artistic Catholicism," which, while not Wackenroder's childlike faith, is an expression of a sincere desire to believe. Tieck's *Sternbald* was inspired by Wackenroder, who had "religious reverence, not only for art in the abstract but also for the individual works of art." It is "a feeble echo of Wilhelm Meister," in sentiment "as widely removed from that singular virtuoso performance as the dim Romantic twilight is from the daylight of pagan rationalistic Weimar." Boyesen, analyzing its plot, cites its moody, lyrical manner, which characterizes most of Tieck's novels, as it does those of Brentano, Arnim, Hoffmann, and his other successors.

Boyesen's treatment of Ludwig Tieck is excellent but is deficient in two respects: it concerns itself only with Tieck's earlier period, and it tends to be rather cool to Tieck because of Boyesen's prejudice in favor of realism. This attitude appears more clearly in his later *Essays on German Literature* than in these articles. He acknowledges Tieck's achievements in culturally widening the national horizon by his translations. He praises the efforts of Tieck, Wackenroder, and Novalis in introducing Christianity into literature, and he commends the romanticists' noble, if erroneous, striving for truth. In the *Essays,* he says of the romantic novel:

> There will always be those who pander to the crude delight in marvels, and there will always be people ready to consume their wares. But let not these people fancy that their delight in these modified fairy tales is an intellectual enjoyment which argues "literary tastes." . . . A higher degree of fidelity, a deeper inward truth, as regards motives, impulses, causes, and effects, is demanded by realism; while romanticism (using nature as a painter does his colors, for purpose of mixture and arbitrary composition) gives yet a tolerably free rein to fancy and refuses allegiance to the logic of life.

Boyesen relies on Heine's opinions in his study of Tieck, quoting from him freely even to the point of repeating his errors. Heine had romanticism in his blood, but he also reacted violently against it. Boyesen himself, in his essay on "The Social Aspects of the German Romantic School," comments on Heine's unreliability but seems to have forgotten it in the course of his study of Tieck. While he quotes Heine's characterization of Tieck's tales, it is hardly fair for him to leave the reader with the impression that Tieck, by becoming "a royal Saxon court counselor" in Dresden, had sold out his early ideals. Nor is Boyesen justified in his assumption that Tieck's fundamental interest in his later life was the theater, because it served as an escape from the grievous political conditions of the post-Napoleonic era. Boyesen completely ignores Tieck's later *Novellen*, the growing realistic trend in his work, and his development of romantic or idealistic realism as his final position. At this time romanticism, following the influence of Solger, was to Tieck a spiritual outlook founded on ultimate reality, toward which he had been groping from the very beginning. Boyesen could have observed this change in attitude in Tieck's reaction to the romantic excesses of the Hoffmann-Arnim group. He could also have noted Tieck's mature philosophical viewpoint and the realistic trend of his later *Novellen*, such as *Vittoria Accorombona*, which deals with so non-escapist a theme as a balanced glorification of woman's emancipation.

There are several other Tieck references which should be cited. In an article entitled, "Gute und schlechte Romane," Carl Dänzer, editor of the St. Louis *Anzeiger des Westens*, August 29, 1875, lists Tieck with Wieland, Jean Paul, and Goethe, as great novelists, and adds a list of authors who are supposed to have popularized fiction: Bulwer, Cooper, Irving, Sealsfield,

Spindler, Spielhagen, Zschokke, Hauff, Holtei, Heyse, the older Dumas, George Sand, and Victor Hugo.

Hofacker cites a reference to Tieck and another Tieck item in his study which I have been unable to verify. The first appeared in the *Tribüne* of February 12, 1881, on the one hundredth anniversary of Arnim's birth. As Hofacker says, it is significant that on this occasion the journal should publish a description of the poet's life and works under the heading: "Ein verschollener Dichter." This serves as a good gauge of the attitude not only to Arnim but to romanticism in general at this time. Hofacker quotes from this article: "Who nowadays can derive any pleasure from reading such men as Tieck, Schlegel, Brentano, Novalis? Like the shadowy figures in their poetic works, they will continue to lead a shadowy existence in the history of our literature." Hofacker also mentions an article in the *Mississippiblätter* of July 22, 1888, entitled "Der alte Tieck" which describes the "last phase of his long life."

In an article in *Modern Language Notes*, 1895, X, 129-31, by Kuno Francke, entitled, "A Parallel to Goethe's *Euphorion*," some similarities are noted between the figure of "Scherz" in Tieck's poem *Phantasus* and Euphorion. Francke asks if it is not "reasonable to assume that one of the most characteristic productions of the foremost romantic writer should have been in Goethe's mind when he undertook the poetic delineation of the flighty offspring of Romanticism and Classicism." He asserts that the *Phantasus* must have been known to Goethe, and that the latter had a high opinion of Tieck. Of course, no literary parallel can possibly replace the tremendous importance of Byron as a living prototype for Euphorion. It is possible that certain touches of motive, such as are cited by Francke in the two works, may have been used by Goethe. But Goethe's high opinion of Tieck must be qualified by what we have already learned about their relationship.

B.

Tieck's Reception in American Books and Text Books Prior to 1900.

The nineteenth century reception of Tieck in American journals is paralleled by his influence in various books and school editions. *Der blonde Eckbert* was reproduced in the first edition of Follen's *Deutsches Lesebuch für Anfänger*, Cambridge, 1826. This presents the text as given in the 1812-16 Berlin edition of *Phantasus* I, 165-93, except for minor changes of spelling and punctuation. [Cf. the note in parentheses after the title *Der blonde Eckbert*; (Phantasus, Band 1, Abth. 1)] This edition also reproduced, with a number of small technical changes, Tieck's poem from *Kaiser Octavianus*, "Die Lilie. Romanze." Later editions (beginning with the second, Boston, 1831) substituted for *Der blonde Eckbert* and for the "Lilie" selections from the *Blaubart* and *Der gestiefelte Kater* and the poems "Frühling" and "Der Verschmähte" which is sung by the shepherd Heinrich to Golo in *Leben und Tod der heiligen Genoveva* and becomes the Leitmotif of the play. The pagination of selections changes in later editions. From the Boston, 1936 edition on, the *Blaubart* selections occur on pp. 116-23, the selections from *Der gestiefelte Kater* on pp. 124-54, the two poems "Frühling" and "Der Verschmähte" on pp. 199 and 199-200. The selection from *Blaubart* is the second scene of the fifth Act; the selections from *Der gestiefelte Kater* are Act I, scenes 1, 3, and 4, and Act III, scenes 4, 5, and 6, respectively. The contents remain unchanged through the tenth edition of 1845. In 1858, after Follen's death, when G. A. Schmitt re-edited his reader as *A German Reader, by Prof. Charles Follen, D. D., A New Edition, With Additions, by G. A. Schmitt,* Boston and Cambridge, 1858, he omitted all the prose selections by Tieck and retained only the two poems "Frühling" and "Der Verschmähte." The use of selections from Tieck in this reader is also briefly referred to by Theodore Huebener in his article in *The German Quarterly*, XXII, 100, March, 1949, on "The First German Grammar and Reader for American Schools." The text follows the original closely.

Follen's annotations begin with the edition of 1836. These consist of translations in the footnotes of difficult words and phrases, rendered literally and in idiomatic English. The most interesting comments are those which sketch the background of the selections from the plays. He thus describes the setting for Act V, scene 2:

> Agnes, the young wife of Knight Berner, called the Bluebeard, had been entrusted by him in his absence with the keys of all the rooms of the castle, each of which he had given her leave to visit

except one. The key which she has just taken out of her pocket was the one which opened the forbidden room.

He comments on *Der gestiefelte Kater*:

> "Puss in Boots." This dramatized nursery story was intended to expose the false taste which characterized a great portion of the dramatic compositions, performances, and criticisms toward the end of the last and the beginning of the present century. The most remarkable heresies, signal oddities, and fashionable conceits, in taste, manners, and morals are exhibited partly in the little play itself, and partly by the critics who are made to take a part in it as actors in the pit.

The "false taste" to which Follen refers was rationalism in the spirit of Nicolai and his followers, which dominated the literary Germany of the time. It included the sentimentality and insipid mediocrity of the middle class drama as developed by such writers as Kotzebue and Iffland.

Tieck's "Die Brüder" was reproduced in Herman Bokum's reader *An Introduction to the Study of the German Language, Comprising Extracts from the Best German Prose Writers, with an English Interlinear Translation, Explanatory Notes, and a Treatise on Pronunciation Affording the Means of a Ready and Accurate Comparison of the Idioms of the Two Languages*, Second Edition, Corrected and Improved, Philadelphia, 1832. The German 'literal' text and the English literal and free interlinear translation occur on pp. 116 to 139. The standard German text is on pp. 183 to 191 of the edition. Bokum remains faithful to Tieck's original version. There is only one rather lengthy omission, on p. 183, after the words "und eben desswegen glücklicher" in *Schriften*, VIII, 246:

> er war bald mit einigen Kaufleuten bekannt, die bis dahin mit Machmud ihre Geschäfte gemacht hatten, und es gelang ihm, sie zu seinen Freunden zu machen: dadurch verlor sein Bruder manchen Vortheil, der jetzt auf seiner Seite fiel.

There are substitutions of individual words, such as, "sie brachten ihm jedesmal reichliche Zinsen" (Bokum, 183) for "sie trugen ihm jedesmal reichliche Zinsen" (*Schriften*, VIII, 245), and minor changes in capitalization or spelling. Bokum uses the interlinear method.

A republication of two stories by Tieck appeared in 1839. The stories are *Das Zauberschloss; Novelle von Ludwig Tieck*,

1839, and *Pietro von Abano oder Petrus Apone*; Zaubergeschichte von Ludwig Tieck, 1839. The chief inconsistency is in the capitalization of the second singular familiar pronoun. In the second *Novelle,* the 'du' and 'euch' forms are consistently printed in lower case rather than with the regular capitalization in the original.

Two other contemporary works, while not concerned directly with Tieck, have a certain bearing on him. The first is a translation by C. C. Felton of Menzel's *History of German Literature,* 1840, which contains a balanced evaluation of Tieck's contributions to a revival of mediaevalism and of German national poetry of the Middle Ages. Menzel disapproves of Tieck's later use of irony. Scattered references to Tieck also occur in the translation, II, 294-95, 303-04, 305-06, and III, 298-300. In this undertaking, Felton availed himself of the aid of Beck and Longfellow. The second work is a translation published by John Owen in Cambridge in 1842 of *Henry of Ofterdingen: A Romance. From the German of Novalis* (Friedrich von Hardenberg) which, according to the "Advertisement," "is made from the edition of Tieck and Schlegel."

A poem, "Die Sterne und der Wandersmann," and *Der blonde Eckbert* appear in Bernard Roelker, *A German Reader for Beginners,* in 1854 (93-4 and 102-26). The index lists "the dates of the authors' births and deaths, together with a notice of their principal works," in order that students may know "to what period the authors from whom selections have been made belong." After giving the dates of Tieck's birth and death, Roelker speaks of the German poet as creating, beside the two Schlegels "jene Revolution im Gebiete der Kunst und Poesie, deren Spuren noch in der ästhetischen Welt sichtbar sind," by becoming "der Hauptgründer der sogenannten Romantischen Schule." Roelker does not mention any of Tieck's works but considers him equally great as a critic and as a poet and particularly outstanding as a writer of *Novellen.* He notes the great fame attained by his Shakespeare and Don Quixote translations. In the excerpts there are numerous slight deviations from the original. The poem suffers particularly in this respect. Roelker makes three changes in only two pages of text. Considering the length of the story, the few changes made in *Der blonde Eckbert* are relatively insignificant. There are also numerous slight changes in punctuation. Two striking and consistent changes in spelling are "jetzt" for "jezt", and "Ahnung" for "Ahndung." Roelker adds "notes at the foot of each page, giving the derivations of irregular verbs and explaining idiomatic expressions." Most of these in *Der blonde Eckbert* are good translations of idiomatic expressions; *e.g.*, "I soon came to feel at home" for "ich lernte mich schnell in die Wirthschaft finden." Very likely Roelker had a personal interest in *Der blonde Eckbert* since in 1853 he read it to Longfellow.

In 1865, I. De Vries and Co. brought out a cheap reprint in Boston of *Die Elfen* and *Das Rothkäppchen*. This stimulated the very interesting review of German romanticism, including Tieck, in *The Southern Review*, Baltimore, 1868, III, 75-99, discussed earlier in this chapter.

One of the first extensive treatments of Tieck in a textbook appears in E. P. Evans, *Abriss der Deutschen Literaturgeschichte*, 1869, 203-05. Evans states that Tieck's contribution lies rather in "poetic originality" and "dramatic productivity" than in the "aesthetic-critical activity" of the Schlegels. He rejects Barthel's high estimate of Tieck as "the most significant poet of modern times." He considers his early works, *Abdallah, Peter Leberecht,* and *William Lovell*, as imitative of Storm and Stress, Sterne, Thümmel, and Rousseau, and he does not consider his romantic period to have begun until his dramatic elaboration of the old *Volksmärchen* and legends (*Prinz Zerbino, Blaubart, Der gestiefelte Kater*). Evans did not perceive that Storm and Stress and Rousseau are themselves forerunners of romanticism. He labels Tieck's more comprehensive creations, such as *Genoveva, Kaiser Octavianus,* and *Fortunatus,* "the finest and most fragrant blossom of so-called romanticism." He stresses the importance of *Franz Sternbald* because of its emphasis on the "religious sanctification of the arts" and the influence which it shows of Goethe, Heinse, and Wackenroder. Contrary to Evans' statement, recent scholarship ascribes the authorship of this novel to Tieck rather than to Wackenroder. Evans notes that Tieck, in his *Phantasus*, failed to reproduce the "naive, poetic tone" of Grimm's fairy tales, with their strong tendency to the "exaggerated and mystical." He does not make clear that a number of romantic works, such as *Blaubart* and *Der gestiefelte Kater,* form a part of this collection. Tieck's interest in the theater as shown in his writings (*Briefe über Shakespeare*) and in his management of the Dresden theater, is briefly mentioned. Despite his theatrical activities, says Evans, his own plays are not suitable for the stage. Despite this statement, Jürgen Fehling's revision of *Der gestiefelte Kater* was successfully produced in 1921 for the Berlin Volksbühne. Evans' views are generally valid, but like many early critics of Tieck, he ignores completely Tieck's later *Novellen* period.

Tieck is also treated in Joseph Gostwick and Robert Harrison's *Outlines of German Literature,* New York, Boston, (preface), 1873, 392-400. This work appeared simultaneously in England (London, Edinburgh, 1873), and the preface was written in London. It is dedicated to Carlyle.

In an earlier study by Joseph Gostwick, entitled *German Literature*, Philadelphia, 1854, a few pages are devoted to Tieck (209-11) presenting some of the judgments later expanded in the *Outlines of German Literature*. There is also a translation of selections from his essay, "The Seductions of Art" [209-10, and a passage on "Social Intercourse" (210-11)], not included in the later study, which is cited as an example of Tieck's satirical humor. Incidentally, Alewyn has proved that "Ein Brief Joseph Berglingers," from which the selections from "The Seductions of Art" seem to be taken was written by Wackenroder rather than Tieck. Gostwick was, therefore, in error in ascribing it to the latter, and this error was also repeated in the *Outlines of German Literature*.

Gostwick and Harrison state that "variety without harmony is the general impression left after reading many of Tieck's poems and prose-fictions." They contend that Tieck failed to realize the union of art and poetry with social life that he himself upheld in an essay like "The Seductive Character of Art," but they do not consider his later *Novellen*. They criticize Tieck's lack of unity in his *Kaiser Octavianus* and *Fortunatus* and single out his *Phantasus* as containing "the best of Tieck's shorter poetical tales." They attribute to Tieck presumptuousness (because he deals with Shakespeare in the *Dichterleben*) and lack of taste (because he deals with religion in *Der Aufruhr in den Cevennen*), but they include extensive excerpts in English translation from these and other works (such as a somewhat modified selection from the "The Seductive Character of Art" and "The True Eckart").

Conant, in her Primer of 1878, treats Tieck sympathetically as a representative of the German Romantic School, paying tribute to his lyrics, his dramas, *Kaiser Octavianus*, and *Genoveva*, in which she considers that he "developed all the leading ideas of the Romantic School." She quotes Carlyle's fine chararterization of Tieck's stories in the *Phantasus* and mentions Tieck's contribution to the translation of Shakespeare, which "clearly proves his power as a dramatist." Like earlier critics, she overlooks the collaboration of Dorothea Tieck and Baudissin in Tieck's portion of this translation.

James K. Hosmer, in his literary history of 1879, discusses Tieck's work on Shakespeare, the old German poems, his translation of *Don Quixote*, his lyrical poetry, and his "marvellous histrionic faculty." Hosmer is realistic in his outlook and criticizes Tieck sharply for what he considers the excessive subjectivity of his productions:

> In a great part of his lyrics he represents the things of nature as personified, making them then speak out the sense of which in his idea they were symbols, following the thought of Schelling. They are often lovely, but utterly arbitrary. They give not nature, but attractions, secret yearnings, and vaporous whims; and corresponding to the inner uncertainty was the form vague.

Hosmer is harsh in his criticism of vagueness in Tieck's lyrics and of the prolixity which he finds not only in Tieck but in other German authors, such as Wieland and Richter. He objects strongly to those of Tieck's characteristics that class him with the Romanticists, such as his "excessive subjectivity, striving to impress his own sense, whims, dreamings, upon the objects of nature." His hostility is further seen in his tendency to quote from such unfavorable critics of Romanticism as Heine and Brandes.

A reprint of Tieck's poem "Zuversicht" appears on p. 152 of Rosenstengel's Reader of 1884. It is preceded on p. 151 by a brief note on the life of Tieck, with nothing about his works or his general literary significance. Rosenstengel apparently used Tieck's 1821 edition of his *Gedichte* as his source, and he adheres to his original faithfully, except for a few slight changes in spelling and punctuation.

Kuno Francke's *A History of German Literature As Determined by Social Forces*, New York, (cop.) 1896, 1901, 1931, presents a rationalistic, realistic, anti-romantic attitude toward Tieck. In discussing *William Lovell*, Francke says:

> The revolting story of seduction, murder, and highway robbery, which as a practical illustration of these principles forms the closing chapter of Lovell's career, would be of little interest but for the fact that Lovell's views of life coincide, even at this stage, with those toward which Tieck himself and his friends were gradually drifting. They, like Lovell, began as followers of Rousseau, they as well as he passed in quick succession from an overwrought idealism to a fantastic sensualism and thence to open rebellion against any kind of moral discipline. And (as we shall see more clearly later) they as well as Lovell took refuge from this hollow libertinism in an equally hollow and utterly irrational belief in the supernatural and the miraculous.

Actually, Tieck developed at the end of his life a form of romantic realism which included a healthy synthesis of all phases of life, supernatural as well as real. Francke considers Tieck not "to have been even a reproductive genius of the very highest order." Such a statement is unfair when, despite his shortcomings, we consider creative achievements like *Der blonde Eckbert*. Although Novalis "resuscitated Catholicism as an organ of profound religious feeling, we owe to Tieck the discovery of what may be called the worldly side of Catholicism." But Tieck is not all Catholicism, since the story is inspired rather by nature demonism. Nor is it entirely true that Uhland's earliest songs are superior to Tieck's in "clearness of vision," "simplicity," and "depth of sentiment." Consider such masterpieces as "Herbstlied," or "Zuversicht." Francke ignores completely Tieck's later *Novellen* period. This is all the more surprising, since he refers here to the thorough study on them by J. Minor, *Tieck als Novellendichter; Akad. Blätter* I, 129ff. To the later Tieck he would probably have been much more sympathetic. Francke notes that the *Genoveva* and the *Octavian* are not real portrayals of mediaeval legend. Tieck's efforts towards the restoration of ancient poetry and art were successful in his *Minnelieder aus dem schwäbischen Zeitalter*.

Wells deals with Tieck in his *Modern German Literature*, Boston, 1897. This work was reprinted in a second revised and enlarged edition, 1906, and again, 1909. Wells also reflects the realistic prejudices of his time against Tieck. Tieck's *Puss in Boots* "had neither the earnestness nor the passion to make it more than a plaything of fancy." Wells maintains that this fault "followed him through life, even after he broke with the principles of the Romantic School, and, with occasional relapses, became essentially realistic." Despite the fact that Tieck had made *Wilhelm Meister* the model for his *Sternbald*, he showed his lack of a realistic grasp of life, a fault characteristic of all the Romanticists, in the artificiality of the characters portrayed and the loosening of social ties. The lack of purpose proclaimed in *Sternbald* serves to show why, "though many read Tieck for pastime, his work, especially in this earlier romantic period, lacks claim to a permanent place in literature, and was indeed dead before his death." Apart from his prejudice, Wells commits a serious error of fact. There is no evidence that while Tieck was a student, he "wrote student-songs destined to outlive his riper work."

Chapter Three

AMERICAN TRANSLATIONS OF TIECK

Tieck's works were translated in America in considerable numbers. These translations appeared chiefly in journals and school editions. "The Love-Charm. A Tale from the German of Tieck" was published in the *New-York Literary Gazette, and Phi Beta Kappa Repository*, January 7, 1826, 274-80. It is an accurate and skillful translation, with only a few omissions. Two poems are reprinted in later numbers of the *Repository*, the one dealing with ball-music on January 14, 1826, 297-98, entitled, "Written After a Masquerade Ball," and one in the January 21, 1826 number of the *Repository*, 312-13, as "Stanzas (from the German of Tieck)." In *Ludwig Tieck's Schriften* these poems occur in Volume IV, 263-65, and Volume IV, 248-49. Goodnight, 156, lists only the poem printed on p. 312 of this journal but not the preceding one on pp. 297-98. The translator skillfully retains the meaning of the original, yet he adds an English spirit by using such expressions as "lengthening and ever lengthening" for "länger und länger" or "lifeless limbs" for "mit aufgelösten Gliedern" and by handling the German participial phrase "zugeführt zu haben" as a relative clause or *vice versa*.

Of the two poems the first is more difficult to translate because of its wildly despondent mood and complicated metric system. The translator has preserved the meaning of the original, the only serious blunder being the translation of "Klee" by "clay." There is some padding in the introduction of the lines, "Like arrows, keen and numberless" and "To leave the victim slumberless, And drag forth poisoned madness" and in the repetition of the line, "And cries, Wild Spirit, awake!" The second poem preserves the metre, the meaning, and the aesthetic effect of the original more completely.

In the *Museum of Foreign Literature and Science*, July to December, 1830, XVII, 283-85, there appeared a reprint from the *New Monthly Magazine*, "Specimens of German Genius." The excerpt on Tieck presents an abridgment of the famous analogy between a feast and a drama which occurs in Tieck's *Phantasus* (*Schriften*, IV, 58-71) and was later republished by Sarah Austin in her *Fragments from German Prose Writers*,

London, 1841, 111-20. Since Mrs. Austin's work appeared originally in England, and this and her other translations are discussed by Professor Zeydel in his *Ludwig Tieck and England*, 201f. it is not necessary for us to analyze it here.

A rendering of the first part of the *Dichterleben* appeared in *The New-York Atlas Magazine* for July 1 and July 15, 1834 (Nos. 13 and 14), 193-202 and 209-17. The German text is based on pertinent excerpts from *Schriften*, XVIII, *Dichterleben*, Erster Theil, 47-170. There are only a few inaccuracies. "In Blei gefassten Scheiben" is translated as "oval panes" (193); "und kräftigen, freundlichen Lippen" as "and decisive but small lips" (193); "those secretaries" (209) is a definite error for "diese Sectirer;" "angrily smilling" (*sic*) (212) is scarcely "freundlich zürnend;" "the inspired writer" (215) scarcely does justice to "der Selige;" "with broken eyes" (217) is a mistranslation for "mit brechendem Auge." Apart from these minor errors the translation is effective in view of its extensiveness.

In *The Knickerbocker, or New York Monthly Magazine*, New York, 1840, XV, 331, there appeared a poem, "Spring In Imitation of the German of Tieck," signed "H. C. W." Despite considerable research I have been unable to find any poem by Tieck which it might resemble. Its composition was probably influenced by the inclusion of a poem by Tieck entitled "Frühling" in Follen's very popular *Deutsches Lesebuch für Anfänger* from 1831 on. The poem appeared in the Boston, 1831, edition of this *Lesebuch*, 239, in the later editions of 1836 or 1839 on p. 199, as well as in the tenth, 1845, edition on the same page, and even in a posthumous revised edition of 1858. A later translation by Charles T. Brooks of a poem on the same subject, which appeared in Boston and London, 1842, was, we may safely assume, definitely based on this source.

A translation by J. L. Motley of the *Blue Beard* appeared in *The New World*, Vol. I, New York, December 19 and December 26, 1840 (Nos. 29 and 30). No. 29 contains the first two acts on pp. 449 to 452; the remaining three acts appear on pp. 478 to 483 in No. 30. The "Advertisement" reveals the contemporary attitude to Tieck. The editors seem to be familiar only with the early Tieck, ignoring completely his production after 1821. The preface points out that although the name of Tieck is familiar to the American reader, only a few of his works have been translated into English. Therefore, this specimen is offered to the readers of *The New World*. Tieck is described as "the most popular living author of Germany; his writings are upon a variety of subjects, and his critical essays, particularly upon topics connected with the fine arts, rank very high in European literature." But his popularity "is chiefly derived from his lighter work ... His tales, poems and satires, are considered by his countrymen to be full of wit, humor, and a lively fancy, and have procured for him the title of the German Boccaccio." *Bluebeard* has been selected to determine "whether his writings will please the American public or not." It is described as "one of the series entitled Fantasie"—a rather poor translation for *Phantasus*. This work resembles the set in being "a dramatised nursery tale, in which the plot is artificially arranged to be sure, but which is chiefly entertaining as being the vehicle for the author's delicate humor, satire and romance."

The translation is both accurate and idiomatic. Compare these renderings:

> Freilich, und der sitzt ihm an einem verhenkerten Gesichte, an einer wahren Galgen-Physiognomie.

> Yes indeed; and that, too, upon a hang-dog face, upon a veritable, gallows physiognomy.

> Peter. Verfluchte Neugier!—Er wirft zornig den Schlüssel hin. Durch dich kam die erste Sünde in die unschuldige Welt, und immer noch lenkst du den Menschen zu ungeheuren Verbrechen, die oft zu schwarz und greulich sind, um nur genannt zu werden.

> Hugo [Motley has changed "Peter" to "Hugo"] Accursed curiosity! (throwing down the key in a passion.) Through thee came the first sin into the innocent world, and still dost thou decoy mankind to monstrous crimes which are often too black and dreadful to be named.

This skill is also apparent in his translation of the song sung by Agnes in Act II:

> Rosen und Nelken
>   Bekränzen das Haupt,
> Und ach! sie verwelken,
>   Der Baum steht entlaubt;
> Der Frühling, er scheidet,
>   Macht Winter zum Herrn,
> Die Liebe vermeidet
>   Und fliehet so fern.

> Carnations and roses
>   Were wreathed on my head,
> But ah! how soon withered!
>   Those garlands are dead—
> The summer departing
>   Leaves Winter her sway;
> And Love spreads his pinions
>   And flies far away.

This poem was reprinted with only slight changes in punctuation, and the substitution of "has departed" for "hath departed" in *Harper's New Monthly Magazine,* June to November, 1877, LV, 611-12, under the title, "Waifs from Motley's Pen." This translation is not inferior to the one included by Longfellow in his anthology and has the added merit of being more faithful to the rime-scheme of the original.

Two long passages are translated in *The Ladies' Companion,* XIII, June, 1840, in Mrs. E. F. Ellet's article on "German Novelists." The first, on p. 87, is taken from *Musikalische Leiden und Freuden* and deals chiefly with the effect on one of the characters of Mozart's *Don Giovanni* (*Schriften,* XVII, 324). The second, on p. 88, is the section from *Die Reisenden* in which Wolfsberg is introduced to a madhouse and its inhabitants and their vagaries are described at length (*Schriften,* XVII, 192-96). There are such excellent translations as "For my part, it seemed during the overture as if all my senses were enthralled," for "Mir aber war, als fiele mir schon während der Ouvertüre eine Binde von allen Sinnen." The translator's skill in breaking up the complex German sentence structure appears in the translation of the passage from *Die Reisenden*:

> Sie traten in den untern grossen Saal, und Wolfsberg, der so lange in der Einsamkeit und im kleinen Zimmer gelebt hatte, war so vom Licht, von der Gesellschaft und dem weiten Blicke über die Ebne und das Waldgebirge hin geblendet, dass er sich nur schwer fassen konnte, und einige Zeit brauchte, um sich mit allen diesen Gegenständen, vorzüglich aber mit den Menschen in dem grossen Gemache bekannt zu machen.
>
> They descended to the great Hall. Wolfsberg, from having been shut up so long in his little chamber, was half blinded by the light, by the company—and the prospect of plain and mountain opened on his view from the windows. He could not at once collect himself, and required time to become familiar with the objects before him.

A translation of *The Klausenburg*, also by Mrs. E. F. Ellet, appeared in *The United States Magazine, and Democratic Review*, New Series, New York, 1844, XIV, 501-10, with the footnote: "This is not a translation of Tieck's story, on which, however, it is founded." It is merely a paraphrase of the plot as given by Tieck, omitting the frame-story, most of its characters, and all of its dialogue. The wife is not named Lillian but Elisabeth. This rendering cannot be considered a formal translation.

Die Freunde appeared under the title of *The Friends* in *The United States Magazine, and Democratic Review*, New York, May, 1845, XVI, 496-501. There are a few defects: "peasants" (396, *i.e.*, 496) for "Bäuerinnen" (*Schriften*, Berlin, 1829, XIV, 143); "one other question" (500) for "noch zwei Fragen" (156); a juxtaposition like "thy nobler aspirations and fancies are debased" (500) for "(Du hast) . . . Deinen menschlichen Empfindungen Phantasien untergeschoben" (157). Generally, however, the translation is excellent:

> Der muntre Sonnenschein glänzte in den hellgrünen Gebüschen; die Vögel zwitscherten und sprangen hin und wieder; die fröhlichen Lerchen sangen über den leichten, vorüberfliegenden Wolken! Düfte kamen von den frischen Wiesen und alle Obstbäume in den Gärten blühten weiss und freundlich.

> The glad sunshine brightened with its rays the green grove; birds were warbling and springing here and there; above the light shifting clouds sang the gaysome larks; a fragrance came from the fresh meadows, and white and beautiful bloomed the fruit trees in the gardens.

The Southern Quarterly Review, October, 1844, VI, 428ff. devotes considerable space to Tieck and presents two specimens from the story "Pietro von Abano" (430-32). Another translation, "The Superfluities of Life . . . A Tale Abridged from Tieck" appeared in *The Southern Literary Messenger*, 1845, XI, 720-27, as a reprint from *Blackwood's Magazine*, February, 1845. As an English translation, it is discussed by Professor Zeydel in his *Ludwig Tieck and England*, 199ff.

In 1848 appeared Frederic H. Hedge's *Prose Writers of Germany*, containing a biographical sketch of Tieck and a translation of his *Elves*. Hedge says: "The following notice, as well as the translation from Tieck, is from Carlyle 'German Romance'." Kuno Francke and William G. Howard, who reprinted this translation in their *The German Classics of the Nineteenth and Twentieth Centuries*, New York, cop. 1913, IV, 272-93, state that *The Elves*, translated by Hedge, is reprinted by "Permission Porter and Coates, Philadelphia." The translation is, therefore, not an independent one. A comparison of Hedge's and Carlyle's versions shows a considerable number of changes in spelling, punctuation, and phrasing, but no vital departure from Carlyle. Carlyle's translations of Tieck exerted a strong influence on American translators, as can be seen in the Fiske translation of *The Fair-Haired Eckbert* discussed below, although the indebtedness of the translator is not openly acknowledged.

In *The Southern Literary Messenger*, Richmond, 1850, XVI, 217-21, there appeared a translation of Tieck's "Die Brüder" entitled "The Brothers. A Version from the German of Tieck." The translation suffers from rather extensive padding. Bokum's *Interlinear German Reader*, Philadelphia, 1832, contains a German reprint of this Novelle, together with both a literal interlinear translation and interpolations of equivalent idiomatic phrases freely translated into English. This is followed by the German text. Whether or not the selection of this *Novelle* by the translator was influenced by this reader remains a matter of conjecture.

"Evening Talk," which appeared in *The Knickerbocker, or The New-York Monthly Magazine*, New York, 1854, XLIV, 253-61, is also excessively padded:

> Das ist die einzige Gespenstergeschichte, die ich erlebt habe.

> And this is the nearest approach to a ghost-story which I can relate to you from my own experience; although I confess that I still cherish the hope that in some unprepared moment I may be visited by a veritable revenant.

Elsewhere the translation is more skillful. Note how the somewhat redundant reference in the original to bad stomachs resulting from sour beer is omitted:

> Es wäre freilich (eine Gespenster-Geschichte oder Wirthshaus-Erscheinung), wenn alle jene eingegangenen niederträchtigen Schenken, in welchen nur saures Bier zu haben war, als Revenants noch einmal wieder auftauchen sollten, weil sie keine Ruhe im Grabe hätten, aus Angst der Erinnerung, wie viele arme Wandersleute sich in ihren schmutzigen Stuben vormals den Magen verdorben haben.

"At any rate, you must confess," said the Lieutenant, "that it would be rather 'frightful' if all the miserable little ale-houses at which we may have chanced to drink sour beer in our lives should be continually coming back to haunt us."

In 1854 appeared Baskerville's *The Poetry of Germany*. Text and translation are printed on opposite sides of the page. *The Ridpath Library of Universal Literature*, XXIII, New York, 1898, reprints the "Autumn Song" and "Confidence" as given in this edition, pp. 166 and 167, with only a few minor changes of punctuation and capitalization. The anthology contains the following poems by Tieck and their translations: "Magelone," translation "Magelone" (163-64); "Trauer," translation "Sorrow" (165); "Herbstlied," translation "Autumn Song" (166); "Zuversicht," translation "Confidence" (167). As English translations, these are discussed by Zeydel in his *Tieck and England*, 185, 215f. Zeydel considers Baskerville the best of Tieck's translators of lyrics.

"The Seven Year's Race. A Beautiful Fairy Tale, Translated from the German of Tieck," is an excellent abridged rendering of *Die Elfen*. It appeared in *Graham's Illustrated Magazine of Literature, Romance, Art, and Fashion*, Philadelphia, 1856, XLIX, 228-34. I have found only one serious error: "and Mary had a longing for the red cherries" (228) for "und das kleine Mädchen langte begierig nach den rothen Kirschen (*Schriften*, IV, 365), in which the meaning of the verb "langen," which literally means "reached after" is confused with the English cognate. This was, of course, an older meaning of the verb, as in the song sung by Klärchen in *Egmont*, Act III, the phrase, "Langen Und bangen In schwebender Pein;" . . .

The Token; A Christmas and New-Years Gift, New York, 1857, contains a translation of Tieck's "The Klausenburg" (39-103). The editor of this annual was not concerned with original matter but with the collection of "some of the most charming stories which have appeared, from time to time, as bright scintillations of genius, in the preëminently beautiful literature of Germany." The major part of the work is composed of translations from the German "since the history of Literature presents but few names worthy of being ranked with JEAN PAUL, LUDWIG TIECK, HAUFF, HOFFMANN, etc., etc.!" C. A. Feiling appends a note to his translation of "The Klausenburg," in *Tales from the German comprising specimens from the most celebrated authors,* which appears in almost identical form in this version in *The Token*. Comparison of the two translations confirms that the one in *The Token* is a reprint. A discussion of the merits of the original may be found in Zeydel, *Tieck and England,* 202ff.

A good translation of an excerpt from the 'Garden of Poesy' in *Prinz Zerbino* in which Cervantes is introduced appeared in an article on romanticism in *The Southern Review,* Baltimore, 1868, III, 88-91. The translation is occasionally marred by clumsiness: "A swarmery of fantasticalities I would rather call it."

A translation of "Autumn Song" was printed in *The Eclectic Magazine of Foreign Literature, Science, and Art,* New Series, XXXII, July to December, 1880, 512. Though without much inspiration, the rendering is faithful and shows only a minimum of padding. The second last line, "For Love there is no such thing;" is a complete insertion. On the other hand, "And sang, as he saw my falling tears" for "Es sah mein tränend Angesicht und sang:" is a particularly good translation. The poem takes too many liberties with the rhythmic pattern of the original, substituting anapests and amphibrachs with an intermixture of iambs for the regular iambic and the concluding spondaic and dactylic lines. The translator signs himself, "L.T.M." I have, however, been unable to identify these initials.

Frederic Henry Hedge's *Hours with German Classics,* Boston, 1886, contains a good sketch of Tieck's life. There are a number of errors, such as his statements that Tieck spent two years in England from 1817 to 1819, when he actually spent only eight weeks there in 1817, and that on his final sojourn in Berlin he organized a Shakespeare theater, whereas Tieck also concerned himself with the production of plays by other authors, such as Sophocles' *Antigone,* Euripides' *Medea,* and *The Frogs* by Aristophanes. Tieck's later *Novellen* period is, as usual, disregarded.

The translation in this volume is a selection from *Die Denkwürdige Geschichtschronik der Schildbürger,* which Hedge calls "a hit at Kotzebue and the popular drama of the day." It also satirizes politics and other matters. There are considerable omissions from the original text, such as chapters IX, X, XI, XII of the story (*Schriften,* IX, 58-64). The passage on the anarchic government of the Schildbürger is greatly abbreviated and freely paraphrased (Hedge, 471; *Schriften,* 65-67), but the translation as a whole is a very good one: "nachdem er über die Thorheit der Einwohner noch viel gelacht hatte" (*Schriften,* 70) is translated as "much amused by the folly of the inhabitants" (Hedge, 473).

A good deal of space is also devoted to Tieck in Volume XXV, 14943-60, of the *Library of the World's Best Literature Ancient and Modern,* which appeared about 1897. The study of Tieck was written, to judge by the list of editors of the Advisory Council, by Professor Willard Fiske of Cornell University. I have found only two errors of fact. Tieck did not make "many journeys to Italy" but only one, from 1805 to 1806, and the Schlegel-Tieck translation was not completed in 1811 but in 1833. Moreover, Count Baudissin should be mentioned with Tieck's daughter Dorothea as contributing translators. Köpke's biography is "valuable," but it can hardly be said to be "reliable," especially in view of Zeydel's definitive work. Fiske's summary is balanced and just and merits quotation:

> Ludwig Tieck's was a complex nature that felt keenly, and in turn affected, the thought tendencies of his time. Owing to this sensitiveness to the varied culture to which he subjected himself, he differed much at different points in his development: now he is rationalistic and skeptical, now sentimental and rhapsodical. He played a considerable rôle in that most interesting romantic revival in German, which was only a part of the larger European return to romanticism in reaction from the classicism, narrow formality, and prosing, of the eigtheenth century. His most lasting contribution to the literature of the fatherland will be found in his noble translations, and the fantasies he wove out of the raw stuff of the old traditions and folk legends.

His opinion of Tieck's prose fairy tales is also accurate:

> He (Tieck) was in his prose fairy tales in the broad sense a poet; that is, a writer of imaginative literature (what the Germans call *dichter*), and found in those tales his truest medium. The faults of Tieck's idyls and fantasies are those of construction: he lacked condensation and the sense of plastic form.

Fiske prints a translation of *The Fair-Haired Eckbert* as an example of Tieck's work. This is probably Tieck's best single work of his early period, but it is regrettable that the source of this translation is not acknowledged. This translation is unquestionably that under the same title in Vol. I of Carlyle's

Tales by Musaeus, Tieck, Richter, first published in 1827 and reprinted in the New York edition of 1874, 169-85. Fiske says that "Thomas Carlyle in 1827 made Tieck and other German literary leaders known to the English public by publishing his 'German Romance'." But this can hardly justify an almost verbatim reproduction of the Carlyle translation without any further acknowledgment. The only changes that I could discover after a careful examination of the two texts were three omissions: the paragraph in Carlyle beginning, "There are hours in which a man feels grieved" and ending with "from the countenance of the other;" the paragraphs in Carlyle beginning with "Eckbert felt relieved and calmed" and ending with the words "Walther and the old woman;" and the paragraph beginning "To dissipate his feelings" and ending with "actual history of a living man." The other changes, in spelling, punctuation, or wording, are very slight, but the dependence of Fiske's version on that of Carlyle is obvious.

A number of excerpts from Tieck's works is contained in *The Ridpath Library of Universal Literature*, XXIII, New York, 1898. The editor gives an account of Tieck's life and works, stating that during much of the second quarter of the century he was held to be the foremost man of letters. He prints Charles T. Brooks' translation of Tieck's poem, entitled "Spring" in about half a page. A. Baskerville's translation of the poems, "Autumn's Song" and "Confidence," also appear. About a page is devoted to a rather free translation of selections from "Ein Brief Joseph Berglingers" in the *Phantasien über die Kunst* (which Tieck, in the edition of the *Phantasien* for 1814, ascribed to Wackenroder). These selections are entitled "The Seductive Character of Art." There is also a bit from the *Insurrection in the Cévennes*, "The Camisard Conventicle," about a page in length, with the editorial comment:

> The best of Tieck's novels, on the whole, is the *Insurrection in the Cévennes*, excited by "the Dragonnades" set on foot by Louis XIV. of France. The story is told by a person who had made his way as a spy into a Camisard conventicle, and becomes mysteriously converted to that faith.

CHAPTER FOUR

TIECK AND AMERICAN AUTHORS

This chapter concerns the relation of Tieck to various American authors. In some cases this relation was slight, expressing itself merely in occasional references or in a chance contact; in others it was extensive and had a significant effect on the American's work.

The first American author concerned is Washington Irving. Tieck possibly had a secondary influence upon him. From the beginning of the century Irving had read a great deal in German. This included, between 1800 and 1808, either in English or in German, Wieland and versions of German tales printed in the *Port Folio* and the New York *Literary Magazine and American Register*, as well as translations in *Blackwood's*, the *Foreign Quarterly Review*, and the *Edinburgh Magazine*. He must also have been influenced by the books he found in Scott's library, which contained more than three hundred volumes of German literature, including Bürger, Fouqué, Grimm, Tieck, and Hoffmann. His progress in the German language was "snaillike." Yet by 1819 he had struggled with the originals of Otmar, Laun, Riesbeck, and others. When he visited Germany, he was therefore prepared to read German in the original. As Williams says, Tieck, "whom he was to know, had used, as one expression of his romanticism, the fairy tale, a form dear to Irving."

Irving met Tieck in Dresden in January, 1823. He was apparently not yet sufficiently proficient in German, since he conducted his conversation in English, while Tieck spoke in German. He reports this meeting on January 10 in his Journal of 1823 from his first Dresden diary:

> Go to M Tiecks at 6 oclock in compy with Baron de Malsburg—conversation he in German. I in English—his daughters very pleasing girls—

At this time, Irving possibly also read some of Tieck's works, for among some undated memoranda at the end of his second Dresden diary, Irving pencilled the following list of German works:

Alladin von Oehlenschlagen
Folksglauben von J. Paul
Jean Pauls Museum

    Frauendienst by Tieck
    Arndts Märchen
    Novalis Schriften by Tieck & F. Schlegel
    Menzel Geschichten der Deutschen
    Schau Sprache der Blumen
    Katchen von Heilbronn von Kleist
    Zerbrochene Krug
    Deutsches Theater von Tieck

? Die sieben Weiber von Blaubart by Lebrecht

    Henry A. Pochmann, in his article on "Irving's German Tour and its Influence on his Tales" (PMLA, 1930, XLV, 1159), quotes this note but makes several errors. He spells "Alladin" as "Aladdin," misreads "Oehlenschlagen" as "Oehlenschläger," omits the "&" and "F" in the line, "Novalis Schriften by Tieck & F Schlegel," misreads "Menzel" as "Mengel" (although he does suggest "Menzel" as a possible alternative reading), spells "Katchen" as "Kätchen," writes "Deutschen Theater von Tieck" for "Deutsches Theater von Tieck," omits the question mark in front of "Die sieben Weiber von Blaubart by Lebrecht," and misreads "Lebrecht" as "Librecht." This whole list is not very legible. Irving had written under the first line, "Erzalungen von Dr." which he later crossed out.

    There seems to be no indication in the diary as to the significance of the list, so that we cannot tell whether "Irving had read these books or intended to read them, had bought them or intended to buy them." The fact that such a list exists must indicate some interest by Irving in the authors. Van Wyck Brooks, in his biography of Irving, confirms this by stating that while in Dresden Irving had read the tales of Tieck, Richter, and Arndt. He certainly would have found it easy to learn about them since Tieck's tales, together with those of Hoffmann and Jean Paul, "afforded the most popular entertainment in Germany during the first quarter of the nineteenth century" and were even read by the Dresden court.

    Tieck carried away a very good impression of Irving, since in a letter quoted above (p. 8) Motley reports that when he saw Tieck in 1834, the latter "spoke of . . . Irving (whom he knew in Dresden, and whom he admired very much)." Further testimony of Tieck's continued interest in Irving may be seen in the rather extensive list of works by Irving which Tieck had in his library (quoted in the Appendix).

Pochmann points out that Irving might have derived the device of the framed tale from the technique used by, Tieck in his *Phantasus*. In his *Tales of a Traveller* Irving uses the same method of a group meeting—as the result of a storm following a hunting dinner—to indulge in informal intellectual conversation and to tell stories connected by means of various comments. "The framed tale," says Pochmann, "is a device as old as Boccaccio and Chaucer, and older; but Irving's scheme to get his stories told, the interruptions of the narratives, the critical comments on the tales by various members of the company, and the wit-combats they engage in, all involuntarily suggest the motivating frame work employed by Tieck in his *Phantasus*, in which a group of men dedicate themselves to the spirit of Fantasy and tell, among other tales, the following most popular tales of Tieck: 'Der blonde Eckbert,' 'Der getreue Eckhart,' 'Der Tannhäuser,' 'Der Runenberg,' 'Die Elfen,' and 'Der Pokal'." Thus, in the "Strange Stories by a Nervous Gentleman," in Part I of *Tales of a Traveller*, a group of bachelors are assembled at a baronet's hall after a hunt but, being prevented from leaving by the weather, they decide to pass the time by telling stories. Pochmann adds that in *Buckthorne* there is "apparently an allusion to Tieck's *Phantasus*." We read that, at Oxford, Buckthorne "fell in company with a special knot of young fellows, of lively parts and ready wit, who had lived occasionally upon town, and become initiated into the *Fancy*." There is some doubt as to the accuracy of Pochmann's comment that this really is "a club very similar to Tieck's." The club is described as a group which "voted study to be the toil of dull minds, by which they slowly crept up the hill, while genius arrived at it at a bound. I felt ashamed to play the owl among such gay birds; so I threw by my books, and became a man of spirit." The group is rather a set of *bons-vivants* than a serious group of cultured men. Buckthorne ends by being badly hurt in a fight with a porter, the sport of boxing being one to which the Fancy greatly devoted itself. Finally he calls the Fives Court "a college of scoundrelism where every bully-ruffian in the land may gain a fellowship," and the Fancy, "a chain of easy communication, extending from the peer down to the pickpocket, through the medium of which a man of rank may find he has shaken hands, at three removes, with the murderer on the gibbet."

The outlook of this club is far removed from that in Tieck's *Phantasus*, with its aim of cultivating the highest culture and its refined atmosphere of intellectual conversation. This aim embodied the ideal of social culture for Tieck, who was, as Zeydel says, "Germany's first cosmopolitan poet and advocate of polite society."

There is some question as to whether Irving actually drew his model for the framed story from Tieck. Pochmann himself points out that the device is "as old as Boccaccio and Chaucer," and Williams informs us that Irving used "this trick earlier (*e.g. Bracebridge Hall*, 430-34)." Tieck's influence was merely to reinforce a technique which Irving had earlier arrived at independently. His use of the name Fancy is merely an echo of Irving's reading of Tieck.

According to Pochmann, there are two other instances of possible influence of Tieck on Irving. One is the story of "The Bold Dragoon," in which the dragoon, after a drunken revel, proceeds to dance with the clothes-press as if it were alive. The illusion passes away and he finds himself "seated in the middle of the floor with the clothes-press sprawling before him, and the two handles jerked off, and in his hands." This bears a certain resemblance to Tieck's *Vogelscheuche*, which we will consider later in connection with Tieck's influence on Hawthorne. Pochmann also suggests a similarity to Jean Paul's *Schmelzles Reise*, but "the resemblance is only a general one, and to assert that Irving borrowed from either would be forcing the point . . . It is possible that Irving's interest in Spain was nourished during his sojourn in Dresden by the enthusiasm for the Spanish past which the German *Romantiker* felt and expressed." Tieck was particularly interested in Spanish because of his enthusiasm for Spanish authors, such as Cervantes and Lope de Vega and his numerous translations from the Spanish masters. But in this respect, too, Tieck's influence on Irving is secondary in nature.

Irving met Tieck and read and admired some of his works, particularly the tales of his earlier period, but such inspiration as he derived from Tieck was not of primary importance. It merely helped to confirm and fortify the tendencies which Irving already possessed and had developed independently prior to his acquaintance with the German author.

Zylstra, in his dissertation, *E.T.A. Hoffmann in England and America*, points out that students of German-English literary relations, following Scott's comparison of Hoffmann in his essay "On the Supernatural . . . " to Mrs. Shelley and to Irving in "The Bold Dragoon," have linked Irving's name with Hoffmann's. In trying to prove direct influence, Zylstra experiences the same difficulties as we do in the relation between Irving and Tieck. There are a number of suggested similarities which point to the likelihood, but do not absolutely establish the fact of such an influence.

In 1826 James Fenimore Cooper was at the height of his fame. His *Last of the Mohicans* had appeared in that year, and the popularity of this and preceding novels, such as *The Spy* (1821), *The Pioneers* (1823), and *The Pilot* (1824), established his literary reputation not only in America but in Europe as well. It will be remembered that Tieck spoke of Cooper to Motley during the latter's visit to the German author in Dresden in 1834, and his readings in Cooper may have led to his 'fantasia' on the Indian worship of the scarecrow in the *Novelle* of that name. A further instance of Tieck's interest in Cooper may be seen in the works by him which Tieck had in his library, as listed in the Appendix.

Cooper's successes made it financially possible for him to realize his old desire to visit Europe in a journey from 1826 to 1833. In the latter part of 1830 he stayed in Dresden. He did not make the acquaintance of Tieck, since, as he says, he did not have a proper means of introduction to him and was unwilling to obtrude himself anywhere. Zeydel's statement in his article on "George Ticknor and Ludwig Tieck" that Tieck met Cooper requires modification. Cooper noted later the great homage which Germans paid their authors and illustrated it with an anecdote about such homage paid to Tieck while Cooper was in Dresden:

> We had lodging in a house directly opposite the one inhabited by Tieck, the celebrated novelist and dramatist. Having no proper means of introduction to this gentleman, and unwilling to obtrude myself anywhere, I never made his acquaintance, but it was impossible not to know, in so small a town, where so great a celebrity

lived. Next door to us was a Swiss confectioner, with whom I
occasionally took an ice. One day a young man entered for a
similar purpose, and left the room with myself. At the door he
inquired if I could tell him in which of the neighboring hotels
M. Tieck resided. I showed him the house and paused a moment
to watch his manner, which was entirely free from pretension,
but which preserved an indescribable expression of reverence.
"Was it possible to get a glimpse of the person of M. Tieck?"
"I feared not; some one had told me that he was gone to a water-
ing-place." "Could I tell him which was the window of his room?"
This I was able to do, as he had been pointed out to me at it a few
days before. I left him gazing at the window, and it was near an
hour before this quiet exhibition of heartfelt homage ceased by the
departure of the young man.

Emerson's relation to Tieck is also of a sporadic and super-
ficial nature, although his contacts were more numerous than
Cooper's. Emerson read some Tieck, although at second hand.
There are only a few scattered references in his *Journals*. In
the *Journal* for 1836 (Wahr notes it as 1837) Tieck and Richter
are contrasted unfavorably with Wieland, Herder, and particularly Goethe, for their tendency to introversion:

> A portion of their poets and writers are introversive to a fault,
> and pick every rose to pieces—Tieck and Richter. Wieland writes
> of real man, and Herder, and, above all, Goethe. He is the high
> priest of the age. He is the truest of all writers.

Not mentioned by Wahr, and echoed in Emerson's correspondence of the following year, is the following brief comment in his *Journal* for 1841:

> The *pis aller* of Romanism for Tieck, Winckelmann, Schlegel,
> Schelling, Montaigne, Dana, Coleridge—men.

This refers to what Emerson considers to be Tieck's catholiciz-
ing tendency, discussed more fully below.

There are additional references in Emerson's correspondence.
Carlyle, in a letter to Emerson on January 17, 1840, mentions
Tieck in connection with a proposed reprint of *German Romance*:

> As to *German Romance*, tell my friends that it has been out of
> print these ten years; procurable, of late without difficulty, only
> in the Old-Bookshops. The comfort is that the *best* part of it
> stands in the new *Wilhelm Meister*: Fraser and I had some thought
> of adding Tieck's and Richter's parts, had they suited for a vol-
> ume; the rest *may* without detriment to anybody perish.

In a letter to Hedge, dated, "Concord, 21. Nov. 1842," Emerson reports that Wheeler sent him a letter from Germany in which he speaks of various celebrities whom he met. Wheeler mentions Schlegel, Schlosser, Paulus, and Tieck, who "had been ill with apoplexy but is getting well now in his 70th year." This is no doubt the letter in *The Dial* for January 1843, under the caption "Literary Intelligence," dated Heidelberg, Oct. 20, 1842. In a letter to Margaret Fuller from Baltimore Emerson praises a "Roman church," calling it a "dear old church," and expresses his detestation on that day of "the Unitarians and Martin Luther and all the parliament of Barebones ... We understand so well the joyful adhesion of the Winkelmans & Tiecks & Schlegels; just as we seize with joy the fine romance & toss the learned Heeren out of the window; unhappily with the same sigh as belongs to the romance 'Ah! that one word of it were true!'" Winckelmann and Schlegel became Catholics, but Emerson was wrong about Tieck. As Zeydel says in his biography of Tieck: "It is hardly necessary to repeat that such statements [that Tieck was converted to Catholicism] are based on serious misunderstanding of Tieck's nature. Not interest in Catholicism, but the yearning, love and emotion of the modern poet with respect to the naïve age of Genevieve, characterize his attitude." Rusk's statement in his footnote to this letter which is based on Hans Hartmann, *Kunst und Religion bei Wackenroder, Tieck und Solger*, 1916, 28, that "Tieck, though he developed a strong sympathy for Catholicism, did not become a convert," is correct. A reflection of the same spirit [rejection of Catholicism as a religious institution, but enthusiasm for its romantic and esthetic implications] is to be found in Emerson's letter.

Another brief reference appeared originally in *The Dial* for October 1843, in 'A Letter,' in which Emerson attempted to answer various correspondents who wrote to him as editor of that journal:

> But passing to a letter which is a generous and a just tribute to Bettina von Arnim, we have it in our power to furnish our correspondent and all sympathizing readers with a sketch,* though plainly from no very friendly hand, of the new work of that eminent lady, who in the silence of Tieck and Schelling, seems to hold a monopoly of genius in Germany.

* We translate the following extract from the Berlin Correspondence of the Deutsche Schnellpost of September.

This statement does not occur in the reprint of this article in Emerson's works [*The Complete Works of Ralph Waldo Emerson,* Boston and New York (cop. 1893 and 1904), XII, 392-404], but in a note. Wahr uses this note as the source of his statement about Bettine and Tieck.

Carlyle reported to Tieck on May 13, 1853, on his trip to Germany:

> Of human souls I found none specially beautiful to me at all, at all,—such my sad fate! Of learned professors, I saw little, and that little was more than enough. Tieck at Berlin, an old man, lame on a Sofa, I did love, and do; he is an exception, could I have seen much of him.

From The Boston Athenaeum Library, Emerson twice took out the two-volume edition of *Novalis Schriften,* Berlin, 1826, edited by Ludwig Tieck and Fr. Schlegel; once on August 2, 1836, and again on September 12, 1851.

These references are meagre when we consider the length and productivity of Emerson's life and, according to Wahr, his wide acquaintance "with the major German writers and writings which were being discussed, reviewed, and read in America."

Creatively, too, Tieck had little influence on Emerson. The one direct evidence is Emerson's poem "Waldeinsamkeit," which by its title suggests the famous poem from Tieck's *Der blonde Eckbert,* for which Tieck invented this word.

In *The International Quarterly,* September-December, 1903, VIII, 97, Kuno Francke sees an affinity between the pantheism he finds in Goethe, Schiller, Novalis, Tieck, Jean Paul, Kant, Fichte, Schelling, and Hegel, and "Emerson's views of spiritual personality:"

> This story of the fourteenth century may be called a symbolic and instinctive anticipation of the well defined philosophic belief in the spiritual oneness of the universe, which was held by all the great German thinkers and poets of the end of the eighteenth and the beginning of the nineteenth century. Goethe, Schiller, Novalis, Tieck, Jean Paul, Kant, Fichte, Schelling, Hegel, however much they differed in temper and specific aims, all agreed in this, that the whole visible manifold world was to them the expression of the same infinite personality, the multiform embodiment of one universal mind; they all saw the crowning glory and divinity of

man in his capacity to feel this unity of the world, to hear the voice of the world spirit within him, to be assured of its eternity in spite of the constant change and decay of visible forms.

Again there is no need of commenting upon the close affinity of all this with Emerson's views of spiritual personality.

If we consider Tieck's outlook and the influence of Solger's philosophy upon him, he shared this pantheism and thus possessed a spiritual affinity to Emerson.

The relationship between Longfellow and Tieck is similar to that between Tieck and Irving. Longfellow made his first acquaintance with Tieck's works during the course of the trip to Europe in 1835-36 which he undertook in order to perfect himself in German and other languages in preparation for his new appointment as professor of modern languages at Harvard on the retirement of George Ticknor. He spent the summer in England and Northern Europe, went to Rotterdam in the fall, travelled thence to Heidelberg, where he stayed from December, 1835, to June 25, 1836, and devoted himself to the study of German philology and literature. In the following summer he made a solitary tour, mostly on foot, through South Germany, the Tyrol and Switzerland, returning to America in October, 1836.

During the course of his stay in Heidelberg, Longfellow also studied the German romantic authors. His journal for the month of January, 1836, gives evidence that he was reading *Heinrich von Ofterdingen,* "wild and singular," with "its strangely beautiful thoughts." He also read some Bürger, and stories by Tieck, Jean Paul Richter, Grimm, Chamisso, and Hoffmann. The stories of Tieck are his *Elves, Rotkäppchen, Runenberg,* and *Peter of Provence and the Fair Magelone,* as noted in Longfellow's Journal of January 1836:

> Friday. Jan. 8. In the evening reads *Tiek's beautiful little story* of "The Elves."—and the childish drama of "Rothkäppchen"— or "Little Red Ridinghood," which is full of simplicity and beauty.
>
> Monday Jan. 11. Read *Tiek's story of "The Runenberg"*—wild and romantic: and shadowing forth the misery brought into the world by love of gold. Read also his "Peter of Provence and the Fair Magelone." It is one of the old Romances of Chivalry modernised, and all together too commonplace. But what pleased me more than these, is *Jean Paul Richter's* strange and fantastic sketch called "The Death of an Angel."

One of the products of his European trip, particularly of his studies and experiences in Heidelberg, was his prose-romance, *Hyperion*, published in 1839. This work is described by Hatfield as "the most important single document having to do with his transmission of German culture to the English-speaking public." It reflects his entire range of studies in German literature at this period, beginning with the older periods and ending with his own time, with particular attention to Jean Paul, Uhland, Hoffmann, Goethe, and the German *Volkslied*.

It is striking, however, that among all this wealth of reference to German literature and Longfellow's evident predisposition in favor of the German romantic movement, Tieck receives merely passing mention in this novel. Thus, on the occasion of a reading and discussion of Uhland's poems, Longfellow makes his hero say:

> Oh, it is Uhland's Poems. Have you read anything of his? He and Tieck are generally considered the best living poets of Germany. They dispute the palm of superiority.

But immediately after this Tieck is forgotten in an eager discussion of Uhland's significance as a poet, whereas the former is not mentioned again throughout the rest of the novel.

Longfellow was interested in Tieck throughout his life. In his lecture notes for the year 1837 in preparation for his course on "Literature and the Literary Life," begun at Harvard on May 2, 1838, there are several references to Tieck. In a folder marked "German Literature," under the heading "Sketch of German Literature (1837 May 19: 7th Lecture)," there is a comment on Tieck's "Little Red Ridinghood." The excerpt bears the heading, "Ludwig Tieck. Little Red Ridinghood:"

> It must be a very strange feeling, when one first begins to think he is too old to go to church: and therefore stays at home on Sundays, and sitting in the arm-chair, reads the Bible in large print.

What gave Longfellow the idea for this comment was the following passage in Tieck's *Rothkäppchen*:

> Erste Scene.
> Stube.
> Die Grossmutter sitzt und lies't.
> . . . .
> Sonst ging ich gern zur Kirche zeitig,

> Doch ich bin alt, dazu krank gewesen,
> Da thu ich im lieben Gesangbuch lesen,
> Der Herr muss damit zufrieden sich geben,
> Eine arme Frau kann nicht mehr thun eben.

There are also pertinent lines in Jane B. Smith's adaptation of Tieck's *Rothkäppchen: The Life and Death of Little Red Ridinghood. A Tragedy, Adapted from the German of Ludwig Tieck.* London 1851, 9, 10. A copy of this adaptation is in Longfellow's library.

On a separate sheet containing a list of various readings used in preparing this course, there is also the following notation:

> Tieck. Minnelieder aus dem Schwäbischen Zeitalter. Berlin 1803.

On March 13, 1838, Longfellow read Tieck's *Phantasien über die Kunst,* which he greatly admired, calling it "a pleasant poetical, deep-feeling, reverential book." In 1840 he read *Franz Sternbalds Wanderungen,* and while he did not consider the book great, he praised the "Claude Lorraine atmosphere about the book, which is delightful." This notation in his journal also contains the rather revealing remark that his "admiration for Tieck, which was never great is rather diminished than increased.:"

> Thursday March 5. Read Franz Sternbald's Wanderungen, one of Tieck's Novels. It treats of Art, and its enthusiasm. Some passages are fine. As a whole, the work is not great. The author breaks down now and then. My admiration for Tieck, which was never great is rather diminished than increased. There is, however, a Claude Lorraine atmosphere about the book, which is delightful.

It should be noted that Mr. Samuel Longfellow changed "never great" to "never high:" "My admiration for Tieck, which was never high, is rather diminished." (I, 360). Professor Dana's comment on this change in a letter to me was as follows: "Mr. Samuel Longfellow has changed this to 'never high;' but I think you are right to keep the original reading. Samuel Longfellow probably wanted to avoid repeating the word 'great' from the previous sentence. Longfellow's original word 'great' obviously goes better with his verbs 'diminished' and 'increased.' On the other hand, Samuel Longfellow's substitution of the word 'high' might lead us to expect the verbs 'lowered' and 'raised.'" On the expression "a Claude Lorraine atmosphere," Professor Dana added this interesting comment: "I cannot help wondering whether Mr. Longfellow may not have been thinking of the Claude Lorraine glass which he had, a curious sort of dark mirror which was hung at an angle outside the window so that the reflection of the landscape in it took on the rich and mysterious tones of a Claude painting—or a Tieck novel."

In 1841 Longfellow advises against Gräter's translating Tieck's *Tales*. Francis Gräter was, according to Hatfield, a German in Boston with whom Longfellow had had associations. In 1841 he had applied to Samuel Ward for financial assistance. Ward had lived in Germany and felt he ought to help needy scholars in this country. He was burdened that winter by other demands on his charity and suggested as a possible substitute that Gräter translate "some short but interesting stories" for *O'Sullivan's Magazine*. In a letter to Longfellow, dated November 5, 1841, he asked the poet for some suggestions but considered "all of Tieck's plays and pieces . . . too long." Longfellow, in his reply of November 6, 1841, seemed to confirm him in his opinion: "Speaking of Stories . . . the best things for Gräter to translate from are Zschokke's Tales . . . His tales I think would please. So would some parts of Hoffmann's Serapions Brüder. In fine, almost anything but Tieck." The pertinent excerpts of these two letters which were sent me by Professor Dana, were checked by him against the original manuscript and preserve their spelling and punctuation.

In 1853, the year of Tieck's death, the following notation appears in his Journal:

> (August), Thursday. 11. Rölker dined with me. After dinner he read to me Tieck's Tale "Der Blonde Eckbert."—a fanciful story.

Bernard Roelker (1816-1888) was instructor in German at Harvard from 1838 to 1856. He was one of Longfellow's best and most faithful friends, both while Longfellow was head of the Department and later.

The presence of the following works in Longfellow's library also indicates his interest in Tieck:

1) *Musen-Almanach für das Jahr 1802*. Herausgegeben von A. W. Schlegel und L. Tieck. Tübingen, 1802. (This is signed on the cover, 'Henry W. Longfellow 1875.')

2) *Ludwig Tieck's sämmtliche Werke.* Wien, 1817-1824. Gedruckt und im Verlage bey Leopold Grund. 30 vols. This edition of Tieck's works was pirated because of the inadequate German copyright laws of the time. (Zeydel says: "Another pirated edition of his works in thirty volumes, published by Grund of Vienna in 1817-1824, was also a thorn in his flesh. The reason for such flagrant injustice, from which all writers suffered, was the absence of adequate protection by copyright. In the eighteenth century a German author's rights were guaranteed only by limited state privileges. In 1794 Prussia finally adopted a defective copyright law. Not until 1837 were the Prussian laws on the subject modified. Countrywide protection was not vouchsafed until the diet of the German Confederation passed a series of copyright laws between 1837 and 1857.")

3) *The Old Man of the Mountain, The Lovecharm, and Pietro of Abano.* Tales from the German of Tieck. London, 1831. (Also an autographed copy, signed: 'Henry W. Longfellow.')

4) *The Life and Death of Little Red Ridinghood.* A Tragedy, Adapted from the German of Ludwig Tieck by Jane Browning Smith. With Illustrations by John Mulready. London, 1851.

Additional evidence of Longfellow's interest in Tieck is the section on Tieck in Longfellow's *Poets and Poetry of Europe*. This consists of a short biography of Tieck, followed by two excerpts, one a translation of a poem, entitled, 'Spring,' the other a translation of a song from *Bluebeard*. Since Longfellow, when he began to edit this anthology, was hindered by strained eyesight, Professor Felton helped him with many of the biographical sketches, and the first version of the biographical notice of Tieck was written in Felton's handwriting. The first version of the biographical notice exists in manuscript form. The difference between this and the text as given in the printed versions of *The Poets* is relatively slight. The chief difference is between the printed versions of *The Poets* for 1845 and 1855, which deal with the poet as still alive: "In 1840, he received from his Majesty, Frederic William the Fourth, an honorary pension, and has recently lived at Potsdam;" the third edition which appeared in 1871, after Tieck's death, changes this statement: "In 1840, he received from his Majesty, Frederic William the Fourth, an honorary pension, and died in 1853." Later research has altered some of the factual data in the notice. Tieck as a student did not spend much time on "history" although he did devote considerable time to ancient and modern poetry. He studied Roman antiquities with Friedrich August Wolf at Halle, and pursued the "study of literature, especially English literature" at Göttingen. It is not true that Tieck "on a journey, became acquainted with the two Schlegels, Novalis (Hardenberg), and Herder." He met Friedrich Schlegel in 1797 in Berlin, A. W. Schlegel a year later in that city, saw Novalis for the first time in 1799 in Jena, and never met Herder at all, missing him during his trip with Wackenroder to Erlangen in 1793. While Tieck greatly admired Schröder and his acting, he probably never saw him act. Tieck's abode, except for longer trips to Munich and Rome during the period from 1802 to 1810, was chiefly Ziebingen, *not* Tübingen, as given in the printed editions. (The MS, p. 2 of the biographical notice, gives this correctly as "Ziebingen" although the printed editions write "Tübingen." Cf. *The Poets*, 333: "After this, he lived again at Berlin, then at Tübingen.")

Despite these errors, the appraisal of the character of Tieck's literary importance is sound. The statement that Tieck, 'since the death of Goethe has occupied the greatest space in German literature,' reflects a similar attitude on the part of contemporaries like Carlyle, Henry Crabb Robinson, Hans Christian Andersen, and Ticknor. Like many other commentators, Longfellow, or Felton for him, does not give sufficient consideration to Tieck's later period, dismissing it with a brief statement that since 1819, he "has written a series of tales, which form a distinct epoch in his literary life." Longfellow must at least have had some acquaintance with a few of the works of Tieck's later period, since in his library is a volume in English translation which contains, besides *The Lovecharm*, the two stories, *The Old Man of the Mountain*, and *Pietro of Abano*.

Longfellow selected two excerpts for his anthology. The first is the poem entitled "Spring," which Longfellow took from Brooks' *Songs and Ballads*. In the material under "Translators and Sources," all three editions give the source as Brooks' anthology of translations of 1842, as well as *The Dial*. A copy of Brooks is available in Longfellow's library, signed "Henry W. Longfellow 1844." The reference to *The Dial* seems erroneous, according to a check of George Willis Cooke, *An Historical and Biographical Introduction to the Dial*, Cleveland, 1902, II, 184, 210-11, 225. This is confirmed by a manuscript note among the material on *The Poets* in Longfellow House which states in part:

"Spring. Brooks. 277," making it clear that the source of "Spring" is Brooks' *Songs and Ballads* rather than *The Dial*. Brooks probably took the German text for this poem from one of the editions of Follen's *Lesebuch* since, according to Camillo von Klenze's monograph on Charles Timothy Brooks, the latter had been at Harvard a student of Carl Follen, who inspired him with a love for German language and literature.

The poem is a beautiful expression of the first approach of spring, and the translation preserves both the content and the form. There are a few changes, such as "advances!" for "aufgegangen," or "revealing," for "angeglommen;" the addition of "to the quivering breeze!" in the line, "To the bird's tread, and to the quivering breeze!" for "Im Zweig der Vogel sich vergnüglich fühlt;" and "glances!" for "Wangen" in the line "Schon färben sich der Blumen zarte Wangen." But there are also inspired coinages such as "And earth, warm-wakened, feels through every vein The kindling influence of the vernal rain" for "Allseitig fühlt die Welt ein muntres Regen Und drängt sich süs dem Frühlingsglanz entgegen," and "Cold fear no more the songster's tongue is sealing" for "Den Nachtigallen ist die Furcht benommen."

The second poem, entitled "Song from Bluebeard" is based on the version given in *Blackwood's Edinburgh Magazine*, February, 1833, XXXIII, Edinburgh, London, 210-11. A few slight changes in punctuation, printing, and spelling have been made by the editor. The Table of Contents gives the source as "Song from Bluebeard . . . Blackwood's Mag. 334." The section on "Translators and Sources" merely lists "Blackwood's Magazine" under the caption "Periodicals European." The clue for the source of this poem is furnished by the following manuscript note available in Longfellow House: "Tieck Song from Blue-Beard Blackwood 33 p. 210."

The excerpt is taken from the beginning of the first scene of the Second Act of *Blaubart*, where it is sung by Agnes. It shows Tieck's skill in picturing various moods of nature. The joyous arrival of spring in the first poem is balanced here by the arrival of autumn and the melancholy mood which it evokes. In some respects the second translation is more literal than the first one. The only striking deviations are the lines, "In the blasts of winter Are the sere leaves sighing," for "Wie rauschen die Bäume So winterlich schön;" the fact that the line, "Die Berge stehn kahl" is not translated; and the change of "O dunkles Menschenleben, Muss jeder Traum einst niederschweben?" to "O, wherefore came the vision, Or why so brief its stay?" The second translation does not maintain its rime and rhythm properly, substituting trochaic trimeters for iambic dimeters and changing the rime-pattern of the original.

Another reference to Tieck appears in Longfellow's introduction to this whole literary period which he entitles "VII. From 1770 to the present time." He subdivides the epoch into three sections and mentions Tieck as belonging to the second: "Second, the union of Goethe and Schiller, the Schlegel and Tieck school, and the modern Romanticists. This period extends from 1794 to about 1813."

Although there is evidence that Longfellow was well acquainted with the early phase of Tieck's work, Tieck did not exert a great influence on Longfellow's creative writing or on his work as a prose writer. In his Journal for 1840, Longfellow flatly states that his "admiration for Tieck, which was never great is rather diminished than increased." We know that he preferred Jean Paul's work *The Death of an Angel* to *The Runenberg* and *Peter of Provence and the fair Magelone*. Tieck's influence appears in the atmosphere which Longfellow probably absorbed as part of the general mood of German romanticism. This is particularly evident in his poetry. Longfellow admired Tieck as a poet, considering him, with Uhland, among "the best living poets of Germany," and Pierce and Schreiber are undoubtedly right in stating that Longfellow's "Golden Legend" is of the same family as Tieck's drama about Saint Genevieve:

> "Tales that have the rime of age,
> And chronicles of eld."

In his monograph, *Professor Longfellow of Harvard*, Johnson states: "Longfellow was probably familiar with Tieck's drama, *Leben und Tod der heiligen Genoveva*." But there was little influence beyond this general one of antiquarianism, and mediaevalism, and the romantic lyrical mood.

In his interesting article, "The Shadow of Longfellow," Fred Lewis Pattee confirms this judgment. It would be unfair to Tieck to say that the characterization Pattee draws of Mr. Churchill in *Kavanagh*, with his unfulfilled longings and indecisions, which Pattee considers identical with Longfellow's character, is "the picture of the true romanticist, of a Brentano or a Tieck ... the confession of a weakness of the whole school." Tieck had a more complex personality, strongly rationalistic, so that, while the trend to romantic musing exists in him, it is only one phase of his nature. The "dreamy mysticism" of the German romantic school had first been brought to America and England through Longfellow. In this, Longfellow resembled poets like Tieck, though more particularly Uhland. The evidence of echoes of Tieck's "Waldeinsamkeit" which Pattee adduces in the "Prelude" to the *Voices Of The Night* is convincing, and Longfellow's glorification of Nuremberg in the poem of the same name is definitely reminiscent of the mediaeval art enthusiasm of Tieck and Wackenroder when they visited that city. Like Longfellow, Tieck as a lyrist resembled other German romanticists in his and their early stages in being definitely a poet of feeling and mood rather than of reality. The two poems by Tieck which Longfellow selected for his anthology are of this nature.

Margaret Fuller's contact with Tieck forms a brief but interesting phase of her general devotion to German letters, a subject treated by Frederick Augustus Braun in his monograph on *Margaret Fuller and Goethe*. It need only be briefly reviewed here. Margaret Fuller became interested in German through her reading of the works of Madame de Staël (she is mentioned as early as 1826), and this in turn drew Margaret's attention to the Weimar circle. But the strongest foreign influence and the immediate reason for her study of German were the articles by Carlyle on Goethe, Schiller, and Richter in the British magazines. As far as her immediate environment was concerned, Harvard was then very favorably disposed to German, this attitude being stimulated particularly by Charles Follen, George Ticknor, and Edward Everett. Margaret, who came from a socially prominent family which moved in Harvard circles, and who for a number of years had herself lived almost in the shadow of Harvard College, naturally came under this influence. Of her own circle those who were most helpful in her German studies were Charles Follen, Frederic Henry Hedge, and, above all, the Unitarian minister, James Freeman Clarke.

Margaret Fuller's interest in Tieck arose only a few months

after she had begun to study German. James Freeman Clarke, himself a devoted reader of Tieck, as may be seen in the record of his experiences in Louisville, Kentucky, from the year 1833, has noted:

> Margaret began to study German early in 1832 . . . .
>
> I believe, that in about three months from the time that Margaret commenced German, she was reading with ease the masterpieces of its literature. Within the year she had read Goethe's Faust, Tasso, Iphigenie, Hermann and Dorothea, Elective Affinities, and Memoirs; Tieck's William Lovel, Prince Zerbino, and other works; Körner, Novalis, and something of Richter; all of Schiller's principal dramas, and his lyric poetry.

Margaret continued to be interested in Tieck during her Groton period and used parts of Tieck's *Phantasus* as a text in her advanced German class when she taught in Mr. Alcott's school in Boston in the autumn of 1836. In a letter in the *Memoirs*, she writes about her work with this class:

> With more advanced pupils I read, in twenty-four weeks, Schiller's Don Carlos, Artists, and Song of the Bell, besides giving a sort of general lecture on Schiller; Goethe's Hermann and Dorothea, Goetz von Berlichingen, Iphigenia, first part of Faust,— three weeks of thorough study this, as valuable to me as to them, —and Clavigo,—thus comprehending samples of all his efforts in poetry, and bringing forward some of his prominent opinions; Lessing's Nathan, Minna, Emilia Galeotti (*sic.*); parts of Tieck's Phantasus, and nearly the whole first volume of Richter's Titan.

Emerson sums up Margaret Fuller's spiritual achievements during the period when he knew her intimately from July, 1836, to August, 1846, when she sailed for Europe:

> Dante, Petrarca, Tasso, were her friends among the old poets,— for to Ariosto she assigned a far lower place,—Alfieri and Manzoni, among the new. But what was of still more import to her education, she had read German books, and, for the three years before I knew her, almost exclusively,—Lessing, Schiller, Richter, Tieck, Novalis, and, above all, GOETHE. It was very obvious, at the first intercourse with her, though her rich and busy mind never reproduced undigested reading, that the last writer,— food or poison,—the most powerful of all mental reagents,—the pivotal mind in modern literature,—for all before him are ancients, and all who have read him are moderns,—that this mind had been her teacher, and, of course, the place was filled, nor was there room for any other. She had the symptom which appears in all the students of Goethe,—an ill-dissembled contempt of all criticism

on him which they hear from others, as if it were totally irrelevant; and they are themselves always preparing to say the right word,—a *prestige* which is allowed, of course, until they do speak: when they have delivered their volley, they pass, like their foregoers, to the rear.

Tieck thus played a role in Margaret's development in German literature, until she became entirely absorbed by her enthusiasm for Goethe.

A most interesting statement appears in the *Memoirs* after an excerpt dated "1836" and an item dated "March 17, 1836:"

> With regard to what you say about the American Monthly, my answer is, I would gladly sell some part of my mind for lucre, to get command of time; but I will not sell my soul: that is, I am perfectly willing to take the trouble of writing for money to pay the seamstress; but I am not willing to have what I write mutilated, or what I ought to say dictated to suit the public taste. You speak of my writing about Tieck. It is my earnest wish to interpret the German authors of whom I am most fond to such Americans as are ready to receive. Perhaps some might sneer at the notion of my becoming a teacher; but where I love so much, surely I might inspire others to love a little; and I think this kind of culture would be precisely the counterpoise required by the utilitarian tendencies of our day and place. My very imperfections may be of value. While enthusiasm is yet fresh, while I am still a novice, it may be more easy to communicate with those quite uninitiated, than when I shall have attained to a higher and calmer state of knowledge. I hope a periodical may arise, by and by, which may think me worthy to furnish a series of articles on German literature, giving room enough and perfect freedom to say what I please. In this case, I should wish to devote at least eight numbers to Tieck, and should use the Garden of Poesy, and my other translations.
>
> I have sometimes thought of translating his Little Red Riding Hood for children. If it could be adorned with illustrations, like those in the "Story without an End," it would make a beautiful little book; but I do not know that this could be done in Boston. There is much meaning that children could not take in; but, as they would never discover this till able to receive the whole, the book corresponds exactly with my notions of what a child's book should be.

Nothing came of any of these projects, since we find no further references to these matters in the *Memoirs*, for Margaret's preoccupation with Tieck was overshadowed by her enthusiasm for Goethe. But her vivid and eager interest is shown by her willingness to devote as many as eight numbers to Tieck in a contemplated series of articles on German literature, including, among other projects, a contemplated translation of *Little Red Riding Hood* for children. Her choice would have been unfortunate. The story is too ironical and sophisticated for children, far more so than the impression Margaret Fuller conveys.

Thoreau is linked with Tieck by Beers in his *History of English Romanticism in the Nineteenth Century*. Beers quotes part of the following passage from Thoreau's *A Week on the Concord and Merrimack Rivers*, adding that one is here "reminded of Tieck:"

> After sitting in my chamber many days, reading the poets, I have been out early on a foggy morning and heard the cry of an owl in a neighboring wood as from a nature behind the common, unexplored by science or by literature. None of the feathered race has yet realized my youthful conceptions of the woodland depths. I had seen the red Election-birds brought from their recesses on my comrades' string, and fancied that their plumage would assume stranger and more dazzling colors, like the tints of evening, in proportion as I advanced farther into the darkness and solitude of the forest. Still less have I seen such strong and wilderness tints on any poet's string.

Tieck's *Der blonde Eckbert* contains something of this magical spirit in the colorful description of the transformation of nature by the setting sun when Bertha first discovers the old woman in the forest. This spirit also is evident in the song of the bird with its praise of forest loneliness. But there is nothing which specifically parallels the quotation. In view of the fact that Tieck is nowhere referred to in the very extensive General Index to the standard edition of Thoreau's Works, the direct influence of Tieck on Thoreau must have been extremely slight, if it existed at all. Such relation as Beers saw might more readily be the result of a common feeling shared by two romantic authors than any direct and specific influence.

The relation of Tieck to Lowell is more definite and more extensive, though still slight. Besides the well-known reference to Hawthorne as a 'Puritan Tieck' in the *Fable for Critics*, Tieck is mentioned only twice in the whole range of Lowell's works. The first reference appears in his article on "Swinburne's Tragedies," 1866. He praises the freshness of the typical characteristics portrayed by the plays of Aristophanes, but doubts whether an Aristophanic drama, "retaining its exact form, but adapted to present events and personages," would be as successful on the stage as *The Rivals,* despite the fact that the latter is "immeasurably inferior" to it "in every element of genius except the prime one of liveliness." He cites the failure of one of the comedies of Beaumont and Fletcher, as well as, in his own time, the attempts by Tieck, which were similar in purpose to the parabasis but took a different form of expression: "Something similar in purpose to the parabasis was essayed in one, at least, of the comedies of Beaumont and Fletcher, and in our time by Tieck; but it took, of necessity, a different form of expression, and does not seem to have been successful." While Lowell does not mention what works of Tieck he had in mind, one thinks of the latter's satiric dramas, like *Der gestiefelte Kater.* Lowell's judgment is not entirely sound, for although a performance of this play in Berlin at the command of Frederick William IV (1844) was not a success, a revision by Jürgen Fehling for the Berlin Volksbühne in 1921 enjoyed popularity.

The other reference appears in Lowell's article on "Shakespeare Once More 1868." In setting up his requirements for imaginative truth, Lowell urges "such propriety of costume and the like as shall satisfy the superhistoric sense, to which, and to which alone, the higher drama appeals." He refers to Tieck's criticism in the *Kritische Schriften* of John Kemble's "dressing for Macbeth in a modern Highland costume, as being ungraceful without any countervailing merit of historical exactness." He adds that a deeper reason for this dissatisfaction might be found in the fact that "this garb, with its purely modern and British army associations, is out of place on Forres Heath, and drags the Weird Sisters down with it from their proper imaginative remoteness in the gloom of the past to the disenchanting glare of the foot-lights. It is not the antiquarian, but the poetic conscience that is wounded." Lowell does not do full justice to Tieck by confining his criticism to historicity. The ultimate question by Tieck in the passage is whether the costume accorded with Shakespeare's conception of Macbeth: "Weiss man denn, dass diese Tracht in jenem früheren Jahrhunderte schon herrschte, oder in ganz Schottland üblich war, oder dass die Feldherren sie trugen? die wichtigste Frage, ob

Shakspeare sich seinen Macbeth so gedacht, gar nicht einmal zu berühren." This implies an awareness of Lowell's demand for adhering to poetic truth in the portrayal of a character.

Tieck criticized Kemble's acting because of his tendency to give Shakespearean characters an interpretation diverging from that which Tieck thought Shakespeare had intended. He strove to liberate the drama from the straightjacket of the scenic stage in favor of a geometric stage with permanent architectural settings which he considered to be the true form of the Shakespearean theater. Tieck held to a high standard of authenticity in his conception of the theater. This ideal, since it attempts to reflect the views of such great geniuses as Shakespeare, is also faithful to the "truth to essential and permanent characteristics" demanded by Lowell.

Professor Zylstra, in a private letter of March 23, 1949, suggested that I trace Tieck's influence on O'Brien in addition to that on Irving, Hawthorne, Poe, and Longfellow (whom he rightly calls "the musically minded among the writers"). I have found what I believe to be some definite resemblances between Fitz James O'Brien's *Duke Humphrey's Dinner* and Tieck's *Des Lebens Ueberfluss*. In each of these, there is an eloped couple, the partners in which are socially unequal. In *Duke Humphrey's Dinner* Agnes Grey is an orphan with rich relatives, supported by a selfish uncle. Richard Burton is an orphan with no relatives at all. In *Des Lebens Ueberfluss* Clara is of noble family, but Heinrich is a bourgeois. In each story there is the same gay badinage in time of trouble. Either various dishes of a sumptuous meal are fictitiously served up and discussed, or there is jesting about the poverty of the food and service. In each story something is burned in order that the couple may keep warm. In *Duke Humphrey's Dinner* it is a wine-box; in *Des Lebens Ueberfluss* the staircase. Each is rescued at the last moment: in *Duke Humphrey's Dinner* through the discovery by Harry Waters, Richard's intimate friend, that Richard was selling his gift, a copy of *Erasmus*; in *Des Lebens Ueberfluss* through Andreas Vandelmeer's discovery that his friend Heinrich had sold his gift, a rare edition of *Chaucer*.

These similarities in motivation seem to be more than accidental. *Des Lebens Ueberfluss* was first published in 1838.

An English translation of this story appeared in *Fraser's Magazine* in 1842. An abridged translation was published in *Blackwood's Magazine* in 1845. *Duke Humphrey's Dinner* appeared in 1855. O'Brien knew another German romanticist, Hoffmann, well enough to be influenced by him in such stories as *The Wondersmith* and *What Was It?* O'Brien could thus have borrowed some of the basic motives in *Duke Humphrey's Dinner* from Tieck's tale.

CHAPTER FIVE

TIECK, POE AND HAWTHORNE

The record of relations between Poe and Tieck and Hawthorne and Tieck is sufficiently extensive and interrelated to warrant a separate chapter.

In his preface to the *Tales of the Grotesque and Arabesque*, Poe disavows the charge that his stories were "permeated by Germanism and gloom:"

> I am led to think that it is the prevalence of the Arabesque in my serious tales which has induced one or two of my critics to tax me, in all friendliness with what they have pleased to call Germanism and gloom ... The charge is in bad taste and the grounds of the accusation have not been sufficiently considered. Let us admit for the moment that the "phantasy pieces" now given are Germanic or what not. But the truth is that with a single exception there is no one of the stories in which the scholar should recognize the distinctive features of that species of pseudo-horror which we are taught to call Germanic for no better reason than that some of the secondary names of German literature have become identified with its folly. If in many of my productions terror has been my thesis, I maintain that terror is not of Germany, but of the soul.

This statement has been used by critics as the basis for denying German influence in Poe's works. Even so recent a writer as Quinn has said:

> The judgment of time has agreed with Poe. The attempt to derive his work from German sources has not been very successful.

Poe himself, however, does not deny that his "phantasy pieces" are Germanic in spirit, nor does he deny the influence of German romanticism in his tales. As far as "terror has been the thesis" of his tales, "that terror is not of Germany," but of his soul. But this does not deny the possibility of influence in motives and techniques by the German romanticists.

The main source of influence was E. T. A. Hoffmann. Considerable evidence of this influence has been adduced by Gruener, Cobb, and Zylstra. This study is concerned with Tieck's, rather than Hoffmann's influence on Poe. I shall not deal with indirect influences, such as Tieck's mingling of the real and imaginary worlds or his use of a frame-story, such as he employs in his

Phantasus. These clearly influenced Hoffmann and very likely Poe through him. I shall treat only direct influences.

Direct evidence of influence is contained in the reference in the *Fall of the House of Usher* to Tieck's *The Journey into the Blue Distance* and the two references to Tieck in Poe's criticism of Hawthorne. The reference in *Mystification* to a Tieck who was a scion of a noble Hungarian family and an expert in *grotesquerie*, is obviously irrelevant. Apart from the fact that he belonged to a middle-class German Prussian family, Tieck rarely indulged in "grotesquerie." This is more characteristic of Hoffmann. The name is a vague tribute by Poe to him. *The Journey into the Blue Distance* actually *does* exist. Poe does not give the *full* title of this work, *Das alte Buch und die Reise ins Blaue hinein* (*The Old Book and the Journey into the Blue Distance*), and this may have misled certain critics. Beers quotes Colonel Higginson as saying, "*à propos* of Poe's sham learning and his habit of mystifying the reader by imaginary citations, [Higginson] hunted in vain for this fascinatingly entitled 'Journey into the Blue Distance'" and was "laughed at for his pains by a friend who assured him that Poe could scarcely read a word of German." Beers corrects Higginson's mistake and explains that Poe had misleadingly referred to Tieck's work under its alternate title. Margaret Alterton and Hardin Craig, in *Edgar Allan Poe,* say: "The work referred to has not been located." According to Goedeke, this *Novelle* was published in 1834, with the title:

Das alte Buch und die *Reise in's Blaue* hinein. Eine Mährchen-Novelle in fünf Aufzügen (1834): Urania auf das Jahr 1835.

The extent of Poe's knowledge of German has been much disputed. Belden takes a negative position. Gustav Gruener, Cobb, Killis Campbell, Van Wyck Brooks, and Professor Mabbott (in a private letter to me, dated April 17, 1945) agree that he knew some German.

Poe must have known Tieck's *The Journey into the Blue Distance* in the original, or at least enough of it to understand the title and something of its richly imaginative content, which, as Van Wyck Brooks suggests, he could apply to the fantastic atmosphere of his tale. There is no reference in Morgan's second edition of his *Critical Bibliography of German Literature in English Translation* to any English translation of Tieck's

Novelle, nor in Cobb for the French. I was unable to find any English or French translation of the above story up to 1839 in either the British Museum or the Library of Congress catalogs, or, for the French, in F. C. Longchamp, *Manuel du Bibliophile Français.*

Wiegler, commenting on the Moeller-Bruck edition of Poe, which appeared in the *Berliner Tag,* 1901, No. 309, mentions two elements which Poe borrowed from this *Novelle* by Tieck: Poe cites Tieck's *Reise ins Blaue,* and derives from him "den märchenhaften Einschlag, den Begriff, dass es am Rhein alte, verfallene, schicksalsvolle Städte gebe." I could find no trace of any reference to old ruined cities by the Rhine in this *Novelle.*

Poe's charge that Hawthorne plagiarized from Tieck is more complex. In his review of Hawthorne's *Twice-Told Tales* and his *Mosses from an old Manse,* Poe states:

> The fact is, that if Mr. Hawthorne were really original, he could not fail of making himself felt by the public. But the fact is, he is *not* original in any sense. Those who speak of him as original, mean nothing more than that he differs in his manner of tone, and in his choice of subjects, from any author of their acquaintance —their acquaintance not extending to the German Tieck, whose manner, in *some* of his works, is absolutely identical with that *habitual* to Hawthorne.
>
> These points properly understood, it will be seen that the critic (unacquainted with Tieck) who reads a single tale or essay by Hawthorne, may be justified in thinking him original; but the tone, or manner, or choice of subject, which induces in this critic the sense of the new, will—if not in a second tale, at least in a third and all subsequent ones—not only fail of inducing it, but bring about an exactly antagonistic impression.

This statement has given rise to considerable speculation among Poe scholars as to the extent of Poe's knowledge of Tieck and of Tieck's influence on Hawthorne. Belden has discussed the problem in "Poe's Criticism of Hawthorne." Poe lacked a fundamental knowledge of German, so that he could not have been able to discover the "manner" of a book by direct reading. But Poe was an editor and promoter of magazines. He must have become aware of Tieck through American and English magazines, "where Tieck was a central figure of German literature from 1830 to 1847." Belden states that Poe's impression of the identity of Hawthorne's and Tieck's literary manner was based on "American Humor," in the *Democratic Review* for April, 1845. This article in turn had been reproduced from *The Foreign and Colonial Quarterly Review* for October, 1843. Poe himself was a contributor to the *Democratic Review*. The article praises the writings to be found in American magazines, singling out such works as Washington Irving's Dutch legends, the Quaker stories of Miss Leslie, and Mr. Hawthorne's *Twice Told Tales*: "As a recounter of mere legends, Mr. Hawthorne claims high praise. He reminds us of Tieck, in spite of the vast difference in the materials used by the two artists." Poe might also have found the article in *Litell's Living Age*, October 19, 1844, (a reprint of the above); the *Democratic Review* for September, 1845, or *The Athenaeum* for August 8, 1846. When the article suggested to Poe "that Hawthorne (who more than any other in America challenged Poe's critical and artistic faculty) resembled Tieck," Poe undoubtedly took steps to learn about Tieck through what earlier reviews had to say about him. That Poe did not become interested in Tieck until this time may be seen in the fact that Poe wrote two essays on Hawthorne (the first of these, a review of *Twice-Told Tales* in *Graham's Magazine*, in 1842, the second in *Godey's Magazine and Lady's Book*, in 1847), but only in the latter does he compare Tieck with Hawthorne.

Belden cites the reviews in *Blackwood's* for February, 1833, and September, 1837, and the (London) *Monthly Review* for April, 1841. If Poe read these reviews without reading the books, he would conclude that Hawthorne's style was identical with Tieck's: "Poe filled in the outlines from Hawthorne, whom he knew, instead of from Tieck, whom he did not know." Poe also derived from a review in *Blackwood's* for September, 1837, the idea that Tieck's legends have "a vigorous moral, couched under the playful cover of the marvellous." The same review asserted that Tieck lacked "vigorous imagination," and, therefore, the capacity of portraying life realistically. But Tieck's later *Novellen* were definitely rooted in realistic experience, while his style suffers from this vagueness. In this respect he definitely differs from Hawthorne.

Poe probably read the translation of Tieck's *The Friends*, which appeared in the *Democratic Review* for May, 1845, since it appeared in the next number after that in which he first saw

Tieck's name associated with Hawthorne's. This story contradicted his original impression of Hawthorne's originality. *The Friends* contains a warning which often appears in Hawthorne's tales and essays against "the egotism of fancy." The lesson in Tieck's story is that the "supernatural craving for supernatural goods" is a delusion created by fairies who are really hostile to human happiness, and should not cause us to "despise the lovely earth with its glorious gifts."

Both Hawthorne and Tieck use such allegory, and Belden points to the great resemblance in "the psychology that underlies the allegory, the practical moral for the conduct of the soul." The translator of *The Friends* gave many of the sentences "a turn that makes them sound as though Hawthorne had written them." Belden concludes that "Poe—not admitted to Hawthorne's laboratory, and familiar only with the finished product; apprised by earlier reviewers of some similarity between Hawthorne and Tieck; forming his notion of the latter at third hand from the criticisms I have quoted; and, finally, chancing upon this translation of 'Die Freunde'—might in all honesty and with very little exaggeration say that "Tieck's manner, in some of his works, is absolutely identical with that h a b i t u a l to Hawthorne."

That Poe obtained the bulk of his information about Tieck from journals can also be substantiated for Hoffmann. Zylstra states: "Translations and criticisms of Hoffmann significantly affected Poe's most characteristic and best work . . . The combined effect of these influences justify the statement that to a considerable extent Poe's art sprang from a journalistically Hoffmannesque context."

There are also later echoes of the tradition that Tieck influenced Hawthorne, such as the one expressed by James Russell Lowell in his *A Fable for Critics*, first published in 1848: "His (Hawthorne's) strength is so tender, his wildness so meek,/That a suitable parallel sets one to seek,/—He's a John Bunyan Fouqué, a Puritan Tieck" . . . "His stories have been likened to Tieck's, in their power of translating the mysterious harmonies of nature into articulate meanings; and to Töpffer's, in high finish and purity of style." (*Littell's Living Age*, XXXIII (April 3, 1852), 19.) Since these remarks appeared after Poe's review, they show Poe's influence on the attitude of Americans toward this problem.

Tieck and Poe have been linked by other writers. Frederick B. Perkins, in *Devil-Puzzlers and Other Studies,* New York, 1877, states: "It would be pleasant to consider the merits of those other German masters of imagination, besides HOFFMANN, to wit: FOUQUE (*sic*), GOETHE, TIECK, NOVALIS and ZSCHOKKE. With all these, except the last, there is no English writer of short imaginative tales to compare at all, except POE and HAWTHORNE; while a few of ZSCHOKKE'S have a graceful genial fancifulness entirely their own." Stedman and Woodberry consider Poe's tales "as ideal as those of Tieck . . . both [Poe and Hoffmann]—and in this they follow Tieck—exalted Music as the supernal art." Tieck did emphasize music as the supreme art. "Liebe denkt in süssen Tönen,/Denn Gedanken stehn zu fern;/Nur in Tönen mag sie gern/Alles, was sie will, verschönen." But to Tieck music is not confined, as in Poe's conception of the "supernal" to "ecstatic sadness and regret."

The relations between Howthorne and Tieck have also been much discussed. Hawthorne was imbued with the atmosphere of English and German romanticism, and some of the motives he uses remind us of Tieck. In *The Birthmark* the search for the absolute, the removal of the birthmark from the cheek of Aylmer's wife, proves fatal. This motive is similar to the fatal result of the search for gold and wealth in *Runenberg.* So, too, in *Ethan Brand,* the locale, the scene around the lime-kiln near Graylock Mountain, resembles that of the Runenberg. Ethan Brand seeks the Unpardonable Sin which he attains "when his moral nature had ceased to keep the pace of improvement with his intellect." Upon his return, he is regarded as crazy by the doctor, just as Christian is crazy on his return from the Runenberg. So, too, one of the characters of *The Great Carbuncle,* Doctor Cacaphodel, the alchemist, resembles in his mistaking of granite for the gem Christian's delusion that a sackful of pebbles are precious stones. Brand's heart had turned to marble which, after Brand had thrown himself into the lime-kiln, had become "special good lime;" Christian's heart had turned to cold metal because of his preoccupation with the "Waldweib" and lust for gold. Turner points out the resemblance between

Eckbert in *The Fair-Haired Egbert* (*sic*) and Arthur Dimmesdale. Both dwell in solitude and are persecuted by a guilty conscience, though Eckbert's guilt is brought on more by his wife than by himself. *The Snow Image: A Childish Miracle* resembles Tieck's *Elfen* in that, when the snow-child is brought by the unimaginative Mr. Lindsey into the warm house, it melts and disappears. In the *Elfen*, through the revelation of their identity to an uninitiated mortal, Andres, they become defiled, and depart from the village, leaving it to ruin. There is also a resemblance between the plot of the *Elfen* and the sketch of March 9th 1853, quoted by Randall Stewart, in which a ramble in the woods produces a transformation in the child, as it does in Marie through her contact with the elves in the forbidden forest. Hawthorne champions a "mystic attitude toward nature" such as we see in the *Elfen*, a plea for greater imaginative treatment of other men.

Other resemblances to Tieck may be found in the romantic irony of Hawthorne's *Main Street*, in which the presentation of the history of the Main Street of Naumkeag in a series of scenes of a puppet-show is interrupted by the interpolation of caustic and extremely *terre-à-terre* remarks by a critic. These are not unlike the interruptions of the worthy artisans in *Der gestiefelte Kater*. Hawthorne was aware of this device, for he makes the showman remark at one point: "Sir, you break the illusion of the scene." Beers suggests a resemblance in theme between Tieck's *Der Pokal* and Hawthorne's *The Shaker Bridal*. The motive of two lovers who through circumstances are compelled to renounce their love until it is too late is to be found in both tales. In Hawthorne the disappointment leads to the woman's death; in Tieck, however, the lovers sublimate their love into friendship. *The House of the Seven Gables* shows the combination of the realistic and the imaginary so characteristic of Tieck's best novellistic style. The discursiveness of Hawthorne's novel, his extensive descriptions, and his long moralizings resemble the style of Tieck's later *Novellen*, though Hawthorne puts greater emphasis on moral questions. There are also a number of similar motives: the deeds hidden behind the picture in *The House of the Seven Gables* and the pictures hidden in the wainscoting in Tieck's *Die Gemälde*. The motive of religious fanaticism which occurs at the beginning of Hawthorne's novel— the first member of the Maule family, Matthew Maule, being condemned to death as a wizard at the instigation of Colonel Pyncheon, the founder of the Pyncheon family—is duplicated by similar accusations in *Der Hexensabbath,* in which Frau Denisel, Labitte, Taket, Friedrich, Schakepeh, Josset, Carrieux, and old Beaufort are at various times accused of witchcraft, or of taking part in the witches' sabbath, and Labitte, Frau Denisel, Carrieux, as well as several others, are burned at the stake. In *Die Klausenburg* the workings in a later generation of a curse hurled by a gypsy upon one in power who had condemned her to cruel punishment, is similar to the situation in *The House of the Seven Gables.*

A number of Tieck's tales in translation appeared prior to 1843, the date of publication of *The Mosses from an Old Manse.* Carlyle's translations of Tieck's stories, *The Fair-Haired Eckbert, The Trusty Eckart, Tannenhäuser, The Runenberg, The Elves, The Goblet,* appeared in his *German Romance* in 1827; *The Pictures* in 1830; and *The Old Man of the Mountain, The Lovecharm,* and *Pietro of Abano* in 1831. It is difficult to determine whether or not Hawthorne had read Carlyle's translation, but the "internal evidence" adduced above, at least as far as motivation is concerned, is considerable. Many of the similarities between Hawthorne's stories and those of Tieck were derived from these tales. Pattee also suggests similarity of motivation in *Die Klausenburg* to Hawthorne, as well as resemblance "in a vague way" of *Die Vogelscheushe* (*sic*) and *Feathertop.* Articles and translations of Tieck appeared in English and American journals prior to 1843, from which Hawthorne, like Poe, might have derived some hints. Although Margaret Fuller, who had been most enthusiastic about Tieck in 1836, had given him up for Goethe by 1842, she probably mentioned him to Hawthorne at Brook Farm. Superficially, therefore, Poe's charges against Hawthorne seem credible. As Pattee puts it:

> One may indeed "liken" Hawthorne's work to Tieck's and even to Töpffer's, but it is doubtful if one may go much farther. Certainly one finds in him Tieck's brooding, poetic fancy, his tendency at times to symbolism and allegory, and his conception of romantic art as the ability to "lull the reader into a dreamy mood." Both, moreover, handled the *Mährchen,* or legendary tale, in the poetic manner and both in some instances made use of the same materials.

On the other hand, Hawthorne was a very independent figure. As Belden states, "He belonged to no clique or school, had so far as we know no literary antecedents with which his work can be closely connected, no master to whom he can be referred. He is an individual as Poe himself." There is little allusion to German literature in Hawthorne's works. Goethe is mentioned only once or twice and Tieck is mentioned only in *The Marble Faun*, (Hawthorne, VI, 47-48; *cf.* Zylstra, 254f.) and in Hawthorne's journal. According to information communicated to me by Professor Pearson from Professor Randall Stewart, there is nothing in Hawthorne's letters bearing on Tieck. If Hawthorne was strongly influenced by Tieck, it is strange that Tieck's name is not mentioned in Hawthorne's critical sketches, "The Hall of Fantasy" and "P's Correspondence." Hawthorne was also not sufficiently acquainted with the German language to be influenced by anything Tieck wrote in the original German. Although we know little about Hawthorne's reading during the ten years of his seclusion in Salem, it seems clear that he had no mastery of German before 1843, and by that time the "manner" of the book to which Poe's criticism refers was fully formed. Hawthorne wrote Longfellow from Salem, March 21, 1838 (The letter is in the Longfellow House, Cambridge):

> I am going to study German. What dictionary had I better get? Perhaps you can procure me a second-hand one without trouble —which, as perhaps it is a large and costly work, would be quite a considerable favor. But it is no great matter; for I am somewhat doubtful of the stability of my resolution to pursue the study.

Hawthorne's decision to study German was influenced by the Peabodys, who were studying German at this time. But his resolution proved to be short-lived, for Sophia Peabody wrote her sister Elizabeth some time before July 27, 1838:

> Mary invited him (Mr. Hawthorne) to come with his sister on Saturday and read German; but it seems to me he does not want to go on with German.

Later she wrote:

> He said he wished he could read German, but could not take the trouble.

According to Stewart, "the extracts in which these statements occur are undated; but Julian Hawthorne places them in the spring and summer of 1838. A *terminus ad quem* is supplied by Hawthorne's departure for western Massachusetts, July 27. Although there were classes in German at Brook Farm, and one might have expected Hawthorne to take advantage of the opportunity to increase his knowledge, there is no evidence that he resumed the study of the language before April 8, 1843. . . . And, indeed, the difficulty which he experienced in reading the table (tale?) by Tieck indicates that he had made very little progress, if any, since the spring of 1838. It is fairly certain that Hawthorne never learned German: there is no evidence to indicate that he ever again attempted to read a German work after he had laid aside Tieck's tale on April 11."

Belden's statement that by 1843 his "manner" in the *Mosses* was fully formed is verified by Hawthorne's slow and evolutionary process of work. "If there is one fact about Hawthorne's literary development more certain than another," says Kern, "it is that many of his tales were created by a process of slow evolution rather than by sudden inspiration." The tales and sketches of the *Mosses* were printed from 1835 to 1843. His marriage in 1842 and his wife's enthusiasm for German thought could not, therefore, have influenced him materially, especially since, as Belden says, he was "extremely independent and self-guided" . . . "in matters intellectual and aesthetic."

The actual extent of Tieck's influence on Hawthorne remains unclear. Certainly, there is a resemblance in motives between Tieck's and Hawthorne's tales, and there is, as Just says, the same "mysterious and yet intimate mood" in Hawthorne's tales as we find among the German romanticists, so that their most severe critics, like Poe and Lowell, saw their similarity to Tieck and Fouqué. Just states: "es liegt die geheimnisvolle und doch traute Stimmung der deutschen Romantik über diesen Erzählungen des Amerikaners, und die meisten Amerikaner, und ihre schärfsten Kritiker, wie Poe und Lowell, haben dies sofort gefühlt, wenn sie Hawthorne mit Tieck und Fouqué zusammenstellten." Hawthorne must have been familiar with Tieck's tales in translation. He could not have breathed the American literary atmosphere without meeting them. But, such motives as the double, the curse resting on a house or family, the buried treasure, and the picture of an ancestor who seems to step out of the frame to save his grandson were the common tradition of

German and English romanticism rather than of any one author, and Hawthorne's style and form are his own and not Tieck's.

Just speaks of Hawthorne as having derived motivation, style, and form (*e.g.*, his preference for the short story) from Tieck. But his realistic style came rather from the English novel of adventure, and his aesthetic independence must have prevented the borrowing of form.

Belden's contention, based in part on Schönbach, concerning the differences in style of the two authors is not always sound. Contrast is made between Tieck's slipshodness and Hawthorne's unity of purpose; Tieck's consistency of mood in dealing with the supernatural and Hawthorne's hovering between reality and unreality; Tieck's polemical and Hawthorne's moral tendency. But Tieck's tales, from his early romantic period, are not slipshod in workmanship; a tale like *Die Freunde*, which appeared in 1797, blends the real with the imaginary. Tieck's stories in his later period are based on a realistic background. The polemical character of such works as *Die Vogelscheuche* or *Der gestiefelte Kater* is matched by the intensely serious portrayal of the *Hexensabbath*, the allegorical trend in *Die Freunde*, as well as a consistent preoccupation in his later *Novellen* period with didactic, educational, and cultural questions.

Poe may have been justified in his accusation on the basis of his limited knowledge of Tieck, but Hawthorne, with the exception of *The Feathertop*, was independent and was influenced by Tieck only to the extent that German romanticism was "in the air." As Henry Seidel Canby says:

> It is true that a rather typical selection of translations into English from the German romanticists was scattered in periodicals and in book form before 1830. It is true that Hawthorne might have been influenced by some of these narratives, or by the other literature which flowed from German romanticism. But scholars who found possible sources for his tales in German, have been referred to undoubted sources in *The American Note-Books*. This circumstance, and the thoroughly un-German form of *The Twice-Told Tales*, make it tolerably certain that the foreign influence was of the kind which is said to be "in the air."

So, too, Myrtle J. Joseph, in her Columbia University M.A. thesis on *Tieck and Hawthorne*, 1911, mentions certain resemblances between the two authors, but concentrates on their differences.

While there is some doubt about Tieck's general influence on Hawthorne, there can be none about the influence of Tieck's *Vogelscheuche* on Hawthorne's *Feathertop*. The bulk of Hawthorne's reading in German occurred during the period from April 8, 1843, to April 11, 1843. The evidence, as given in Randall Stewart's *The American Note-Books,* is as follows:

> April 8th—Saturday (1843) After my encounter with Gaffer, I returned to our lonely, old abbey, opened the door with no such heart-spring as if I were to be welcomed by my wife's loving smile, ascended to my study, and began to read a tale of Tieck. Slow work, and dull work too!
>
> April 9th—Sunday.—When it was almost as dark as the moonlight would let it be, I lighted the lamp, and went on with Tieck's tale, slowly and painfully and often wishing for thy bright little wits to help me out of my difficulties. At last, I determined to learn a little about pronouns and verbs, before proceeding further, and so took up the Phrase Book, with which I was commendably busy, when, at about a quarter of nine, came a knock to my study-door; and, behold, there was Molly with thy letter! .... Then I took up the Phrase Book again; but could not study; and so bathed and went to bed; it being now not far from ten ºclock.
>
> *Half past5 ºclock.* After writing the above letter to my dearest spouse, I again set to work on Tieck's tale, and worried through (87) several pages; and then, at half past four, threw open one of the western windows of my study, and sallied forth to take the sunshine.
>
> April 10th. Monday. I sat till eight ºclock, meditating upon this world and the next, and my dear little wife, as connected with both; and sometimes dimly shaping out scenes of a tale. Then lighted the lamp, and betook myself to the German Phrase Book. A, dearest, these are but dreary evenings ... When the company rose from the table, they all, in the single person of thy husband, ascended to the study, and employed themselves in reading the article on Oregon, in the Democratic Review. (427) Then they plodded onward into the rugged and bewildering depths of Tieck's tale, until five ºclock, when, with one accord, they went out to split wood.
>
> [The reference "427" is to "Oregon," the *Democratic Review,* XII (April, 1843), 339-359. The article is unsigned. Hawthorne's "Procession of Life" immediately follows "Oregon," pp. 360-366.]
>
> April 11th 1843. I meditated, accordingly, but without any very wonderful result. Then, at eight ºclock, lighted the lamp, and

bothered myself till after nine with this eternal tale of Tieck
... Till dinner time, I labored on Tieck's tale, and resumed that
agreeable employment after the banquet. It is my purpose, poor
little wife, that thou, the very morning after thy return, shall
take up this awful business, and finish the tale, and then lead thy
husband through its bewilderments, perfectly at his ease.

Just when I was on the point of choking with a huge German
word, (429) Molly announced Mr. Thoreau. He wanted to take
a row in the boat, for the last time, perhaps, before he leaves
Concord. So we emptied the water out of (91) her, and set forth on
our voyage.

[429. When Hawthorne wrote in *Seven Gables* (181), "All his life
long he (Clifford) had been learning how to be wretched, as one
learns a foreign tongue," he doubtless had in mind his own difficulties in learning German.]

Thus, Hawthorne was a very poor student of German, and though interested in a tale by Tieck, he was hindered by difficulties with the language and style. Kern shows that this story must have been Tieck's *Vogelscheuche*. He notes Hawthorne's slow method of evolving his stories and shows that Tieck's tale must have formed but one step in Hawthorne's process of writing *Feathertop*. The germ of the idea for the story is a note to be found in the *American Notebooks* for 1840:

To make a story out of a scarecrow, giving it odd attributes.
From different points of view, it should appear to change,—now an
old man, now an old woman,—a gunner, a farmer, or the Old Nick.

The next step was probably the material Hawthorne obtained from Tieck's tale. Another note by Hawthorne in 1849, embodying the content of Tieck's tale and adding his own, preceded the finished form of *Feathertop* in 1852. Kern states:

It can scarcely be doubted that this note of 1849 is the direct
source of *Feathertop*, which was first published in the *International Magazine* for February-March, 1852. But to accept it as the
source does not necessarily mean dismissing from our attention
either the note of 1840 or Tieck's *Die Vogelscheuche*, for it is
possible that all three are but separate steps in a single process,
the last step of which was the contemplated tale.

Tieck's contribution to the story is clarified by a comparison between the story as given by Tieck and the Note of 1849.

Tieck's *Die Vogelscheuche* is a drama in novellistic form.

Omitting its incidental matter, such as its literary satire, and the long account of the elf Heimchen, the story is this:

> Ambrosius, a senator of a small German town, urges upon his neighbors the desirability of beautifying the appearance of scarecrows after the fashion of the Greeks, who strove always to bring art into life and to set up beautiful statues of the gods instead of scarecrows in their fields and gardens. He suggests fashioning them after the model of heroes, famous writers, and the like. He sets up such a scarecrow in his garden. This scarecrow is made of burnished leather and bears a three-cornered hat of leather with a white feather. Ambrosius' daughter, Ophelia, falls in love with it. Shortly thereafter a nobleman by the revealing name of Ledebrinna and betraying other characteristics of his origin, appears in the neighboring town of Ensisheim. He creates a great stir in the place, sets up a literary society, "die Ledernen", with himself as chairman, and proceeds to pay court to the apothecary's daughter, Elisa, with the strong approval of her father. Elisa, however, is in love with a young officer, Wilhelm. It turns out that Ledebrinna is really the scarecrow who has come to life because it was inhabited by a fleeing elf, Heimchen, under the influence of astral, telluric, and lunar forces. Ambrosius visits Ensisheim and recognizes Ledebrinna. A trial ensues during which both sides of the case are fully discussed. Finally, Wilhelm elopes with Elisa. He suddenly comes into great riches and the fleeing couple are reconciled with her father. As for Ophelia, she marries Ledebrinna, who, in animated form, is her first love, the scarecrow.

Hawthorne's Note of 1849 follows:

> Between 'March 16th, 1849.' and 'Monday, Sept^R 17th, 1849.' A modern magician to make the semblance of a human being, with two laths for legs, a pumpkin for a head ec.—of the rudest and most meagre materials. Then a tailor helps him to finish his work, and transforms this scarecrow into quite a fashionable figure. N.B.—R.L.R. At the end of the story, after deceiving the world for a long time, the spell should be broken; and the gray dandy be discovered to be nothing but a suit of clothes, with these few sticks inside of it. All through this seeming existence as a human being, there should be some characteristics, some tokens, that, to the man of close observation and insight, betray him to be a mere thing of laths and clothes, without heart, soul, or intellect. And so this wretched old thing shall become the symbol of a large class.

The basic idea of a scarecrow transformed into a human being is common to both Tieck's story and the Note. In Tieck's tale the transformation takes place by animation through elfine, astral, telluric, and lunar forces. In the Note, it occurs through magic. The scarecrow is transformed in the Note into "quite a fashionable figure." The same characteristics appear in *Die Vogelscheuche*. Here the scarecrow is made of burnished leather, and wears "an almost three-cornered hat of leather," which covers its head, while "a white feather surrounds the latter like the one which marks the general." "Ein fast dreieckter Hut von Leder deckt sein Haupt, eine weisse Feder legt sich um diesen, wie die, welche den General beziechnet." This bears an even more striking resemblance to the description of the finished scarecrow, in Hawthorne's completed version of his story: "Lastly she put her dead husband's wig on the bare scalp of the pumpkin, and surmounted the whole with a dusty three-cornered hat, in which was stuck the longest tail feather of a rooster." Even if we agree with Kern that three-cornered hats with feathers stuck in them "were in universal use among gentlemen," the existence of this identical description in both *Feathertop* and *Die Vogelscheuche* has more than the slight significance which Kern attributes to it. The parallel between Ambrosius' intention to erect a fine statue as a scarecrow and the following excerpt from *Feathertop* is decisive proof of borrowing: "Now Mother Rigby . . . might, with very little trouble, have made a scarecrow ugly enough to frighten the minister himself. But on this occasion, as she had awakened in an uncommonly pleasant humor, and was further dulcified by her pipe of tobacco, she resolved to produce something fine, beautiful, and splendid, rather than hideous and horrible."

The Note provides that the scarecrow during its life should betray some characteristics of its origin. In Tieck's tale, the scarecrow's name is Ledebrinna, a recollection of the fact that it is made of burnished leather. The literary society which Ledebrinna founds is called "die Ledernen." When he is praised, he twitches his bushy eyebrows, while bowing, pushes his shoulders unusually high, and bows profusely with the upper part of his body, not unlike the figure in *Feathertop*, who after being created by Mother Rigby, "made a step forward—a kind of hitch and jerk, however, rather than a step—then tottered and almost lost its balance. What could a witch expect? It was nothing, after all, but a scarecrow stuck upon two sticks."

During his visionary trance Ledebrinna, when touched by books he liked, used exclamations referring to leather. He wanted, when he became ill, to establish a new critical magazine, entitled "die Gerberei" ("The Tannery"). Ophelia learns on her wedding night that the scarecrow and Ledebrinna are identical. If it is true that Hawthorne worked upon Tieck's tale in the gap between April 11 and April 25 that occurs in his Notes, he may have reached the main point of Tieck's story, a literary satire against the mediocrity and philistinism of the Dresden "Liederkreis," the Saxon poetic group which dominated Dresden's literary taste at the time Tieck lived there, as well as against the love of ugliness and untruth in the French romantic school. These latter characteristics are related to the earlier German "fate tragedies" and derived from the arbitrariness and lack of restraint of Hoffmann. The brunt of Tieck's attack on the Saxon group of poets begins on page 162, that against the French romantic school is mentioned as early as page 74, and is developed between pages 249 and 253, so that it is possible that Hawthorne reached this point in Tieck's story before he dropped it. Hawthorne did not need more than a hint for his own purposes, as revealed in the brief but telling remark in his Note of 1849: "N.B.—R.L.R." Kern presents convincing evidence to show that 'R.L.R.' was a certain Richard S. Rogers, a political opponent who was one of the men responsible for his dismissal from his surveyorship at the Salem Custom House on June 7, 1849. Hawthorne was thus moved by personal satire in writing his work.

Thus internal evidence points to a resemblance between the Note of 1849 and Tieck's tale. Even though Hawthorne does not mention the story by name, his preoccupation with similar subject matter must have drawn him to it.

A number of questions still remain. Why did Hawthorne become interested in Tieck in 1843? Why must he have read the story in German rather than in English? How can we answer Schönbach's assertion that Hawthorne could not have borrowed from Tieck because the form of the same idea in the two stories is so completely different?

We must dismiss as unfounded the charge that Hawthorne became interested in Tieck in 1843, as Lathrop suggests, because of Poe's adverse criticism of him and the juxtaposition of Tieck's name and his own. Poe mentions the similarity between Tieck and Hawthorne only in the second of his essays on Hawthorne, which is dated 1847. He could not have known about it in 1843. Nor could he have obtained it from its first mention in *The Foreign and Colonial Quarterly Review* in October 1843, for the material in the *Notebooks* goes back to *April* of that year. As Belden says:

> This would be highly satisfactory were it not for a few matters of chronology which, though he could not have been ignorant of them, he most unaccountably disregarded. The "Note-Book" entry is dated April 8-11, 1843; Poe's innuendo was made in what, even if Lathrop did not know that it first appeared in G o d e y ' s for November, 1847, was yet most plainly a review of the "Mosses," and these were not published under that name until 1846. It was an odd mistake for Hawthorne's son-in-law and devoted admirer to make.

Knowledge of Tieck could have reached Hawthorne through the large number of articles on Tieck and the translations of his work which appeared in English and American journals prior to 1843. This interest must have been intensified by the Peabodys, since under their influence he began to study German as early as 1838 in a short-lived and not too successful effort. His interest was also stimulated by what he must have learned about Tieck at Brook Farm in 1842. The first entry concerning Tieck in his *Notebooks* of April 8 also contains a reference to his studying German and translating Bürger's *Lenore*. Once Hawthorne became interested in Tieck he could not fail to be attracted by a story which resembled a theme that had been germinating in his mind since 1840.

Why did Hawthorne read the story in German and not in English? Zeydel states: "There is no record that it has ever been translated into English, either here or in England." Hawthorne must, therefore, have read it in the original. The story was published in the almanac *Novellenkranz* in Berlin in 1835, and later reprinted in 1842, in Tieck's *Gesammelte Novellen* and in 1854 in his *Schriften*. Despite the limited circulation of the Berlin *Novellenkranz*, Hawthorne could have found not only this edition of the story but two others available before he wrote his comments in the *American Notebooks*. Hawthorne's knowledge of German began as early as 1838. He must have known some German to attempt to undertake a translation of *Lenore* in the same year that he read Tieck's tale. Hawthorne did not need to read the whole of Tieck's story to obtain the basic hints for his Note of 1849, since these occurred in the earlier part of the *Novelle*.

Schönbach's assertion that Hawthorne derived his idea as early as 1840 and that, therefore, Tieck could not have influenced him in writing his story is open to dispute. There is such a discrepancy between the content of the Note of 1840 and the finished story as to make it impossible for the Note to be its sole source. Hawthorne's interest in the theme must inevitably have attracted him to a story by Tieck which seemed to resemble it. The development of the idea in the two stories is different. In the method of narration, *Feathertop* is a concise, compact tale of 26 pages, while Tieck's tale is a very long, drawn-out story of 356 pages. *Die Vogelscheuche* contains extraneous episodes and numerous excursions into the field of literary satire as well as discussions on other topics. *Feathertop* is basically a personal satire expanded into a general attack against sham and hypocrisy. Schönbach was familiar only with the Note of 1840 and not with the Note of 1849. If we compare Tieck's story with the Note of 1840 or Hawthorne's finished product, we cannot find any resemblance. The resemblance becomes clear only if we compare Tieck's story with the Note of 1849. Zylstra notes a definite resemblance between Hoffmann's *Der Sandmann* and *Feathertop*: "That *Feathertop* also is essentially like one of Hoffmann's automata cannot be gainsaid. Hoffmann's Olympia and Hawthorne's Feathertop do not spring from a mere interest in curious machinery. Men and women sometimes came to these authors in the guise of robots . . . *Feathertop* is certainly, like *The Sandman*, published in *Godey's* for November, 1835, in that the automaton is an expression of the human lifelessness and imitativeness which impressed Hawthorne." Despite this resemblance, the basic influence is the one between Tieck's *Die Vogelscheuche* and Hawthorne's tale.

Thus Hawthorne's narrative writing resembles Tieck's in motivation, though not in style. The resemblance in motivation is general, such as one is likely to find "in the air" during a period when the influence of English and German romanticism was dominant. *Feathertop*, however, was definitely influenced by Tieck's *Vogelscheuche*, but the influence was on the Note of 1849, and represented one of the steps in Hawthorne's evolution of his story, not the finished product itself. Here, again, the influence was one of content rather than of style.

CHAPTER SIX

TIECK'S ATTITUDE TO AMERICA

Tieck's personal attitude to America is reflected in his writings as well as in his rather extensive library holdings.

As Lydia Wagner points out in "The Reserved Attitude of the Early German Romanticists toward America," Tieck shares with other German romanticists their dislike of contemporary America for its philistinism and lack of intellectual tradition. Wackenroder felt that with Tieck as his companion he would not feel a stranger even in California. In a letter to Wackenroder, Tieck mentions that one of the topics he planned to discuss at the students' literary club to which he belonged while at Göttingen was "the harmfulness of the discovery of America." Tieck's hostility to America appears also in the contrast which he draws between the commercial nature of Fürth and the "solidly bourgeois, Germanic, artistic Nuremberg." He calls Fürth "Dieses Nord-Amerika von Fürth" but says that Nuremberg evokes memories of Albrecht Dürer and mediaeval German art. He regrets the invention of the compass and the resulting discovery of America, because it brought in its wake, among other evils, Tieck's pet aversion, the smoking of tobacco. His aversion to the machine age also appears in *Der junge Tischlermeister*, one of his latest *Novellen*. Here his mouthpiece, Leonhard, regrets the impending disappearance of the guild system in favor of the factory system, the evils of which—strong class division, materialism, degradation of the working man to a machine, and his attending moral degradation—he roundly condemns.

Tieck refers to America in *William Lovell*, 1793-1796. Karl Wilmot kills Lovell in a duel for wronging his sweetheart Emilie Burton and then plans to leave for America. But his attitude is not that of a hopeful man who seeks new worlds to conquer but rather that of a man weary of the world and full of pessimism, who goes to America to seek death in battle:

> Adieu—Ich fahre von hier nach Amerika. Der Krieg lockt mich dahin; es wird in der Englischen Armee wohl eine Stelle für einen Lebenssatten übrig sein, der sich dann wenigstens noch einbilden kann, zum Besten seines Vaterlandes zu sterben.

There is a brief reference in Tieck's *Der funfzehnte Novem-*

ber, 1827, to the explorations of Dutch navigators in America. In the *Zauberschloss,* 1829, there are two humorous references to Columbus' discovery of America: one to his successful landing, the other to the encouragement of the crew at the sight of land birds when they were about to give up hope. There is humorous reference to the shouting of murdered Indians. In *Der Jahrmarkt,* 1831, the baron Herr von Steinsberg builds an artificial garden to represent the geography and history of the world, but because of a storm, is unable to show the whole of it to his visitors. He has to omit Othahiti and America. Wolf, in relating the end of his brother's chequered career, tells how he first went to England, where he married a Jewess and proceeded to America. The notorious robber, called "der kleine Caspar" or baron Wandel, ends by fleeing to America with substantial wealth and changing his name. Here his change of name may also produce an improvement in his character. In *Eine Sommerreise* (1833), Wachtel half jestingly brings out the superior virtues of Guben to the insignificant person's admiration for the Louvre, the Strassburg Münster, London Bridge, or Niagara Falls. Later in the *Novelle* Ferdinand extols the historical and cultural richness of the German Middle Ages in typically romantic fashion and considers it terrible that anyone should be forced to live in America where such traditions are lacking. In the *Novelle, Tod des Dichters,* 1833, Count Ferdinand remarks that some philosophers claim the negroes are descendants of Cain who escaped the Flood. They are therefore justifiably used as slaves in America because thereby the curse which the Lord placed upon Cain or Noah upon the criminal Ham is fulfilled. According to William Sumner Jenkins, this idea was part of the regularly accepted theory of the Old South in regard to Negro slavery and formed an important part of their justification for it. Later in the *Novelle,* Luis urges capable persons to seek their fortunes in the two Indies rather than in their native Portugal, the strength of which can only be maintained if the property of the state is not divided. There is a satiric comment in *Die Vogelscheuche,* 1834, that the scarecrow, of which much is made in the *Novelle,* had been transported to America by an art dealer, purchased by the state of New York, placed over the gate of the town-hall to frighten away the birds, and had finally been stolen by a tribe of neighboring Indians who worshipped it as an idol. This tribe, formerly one of the most savage in America, has since become much milder and more humane under its influence, "so that from the abduction of this statue a new era and historic epoch will very probably be dated in the annuals of North America." In *Der Wassermensch*, 1834, the much reviled Young German, Florheim, urges that all published books should bear pictures of the greatest heroes of freedom. He mentions specifically Mirabeau, Washington, Franklin, Kosciusco, Danton, and Robespierre. Essling makes reference to a "See-Romantik," parallel to the sea-pieces presented in landscape-painting, which was cultivated then by Englishmen and Frenchmen, and Lucilie, while expressing great regard for Cooper's talent, considers his manner too "weitschweifig" ("prolix"). In the *Weihnacht-Abend*, 1834, Heinrich is presented as having made his fortune in the West Indies—Tieck considered this territory to consist of only one island—by marrying the daughter of his employer, the richest girl on the island. In *Eigensinn und Laune*, 1835, Friedheim, after abusing Emmeline's authority and collecting as much money in her name as he could, fled with her whole fortune to America. Reference is also made to an American religious sect, whose worship consists of taking off their coats and vests and dancing and jumping to the accompaniment of song. The doctor in *Der Schutzgeist*, 1836, comments on the omnipotence and capriciousness of nature, which, while more and more restrained by human effort, still occasionally breaks the bonds of human control. As evidence of "the smallest jests of her wild childish games," her unrestrained power in primitive times, he cites "the granite blocks of a thousand hundredweights, still lying around in the fields, the last wild waterfalls in Switzerland and of Niagara and a few in Norway, which have not yet been drawn in to be made subservient to mills and factories." In *Der junge Tischlermeister*, 1836, Franke, a crazed youth who suffers from the delusion that he is a son of Frederick the Great, would have preferred to be carried off to America than to be brought up among Jews. In *Des Lebens Ueberfluss*, 1838, in explaining to his landlord why he was compelled to burn the staircase, Heinrich Brand points out that he had been deceived and had been unable to receive financial credit anywhere in Europe, to say nothing of Asia and America.

These references to America cover a wide range of topics,

including American literature, history, customs, exploration, and geography. Most frequently they picture America as a place of refuge from disappointment in the old world, as a haven for criminals, and as a place of opportunity for amassing great wealth. That Tieck considered it a barbaric country, is shown by his frequent references to Indians, his veiled reference to the "Holy Roller" cult, and the fact that America's heroes of liberation, Washington, Franklin, Kosciusco, are praised in the *Wassermensch* by a Young German who is held up to ridicule in the story. Thus Tieck's attitude to America in his creative writing parallels the uncomplimentary attitude he showed elsewhere. Tieck had, of course, a weakness for preconceived notions and he rejected all progressive innovations.

Despite his attitude to America, there can be no doubt of Tieck's interest in its literature, its geography, and its history, to judge by the large number of volumes on American topics in his library. A glance at the appendix, compiled from the Asher catalog of 1849, will reveal the variety and range of his interests. There are many items on American language and literature, as well as books dealing with the history, geography, and travels of America. It seems regrettable that with such a large library at his disposal, Tieck should not have formed a more favorable impression of America. But his prejudice against its philistinism and lack of intellectuality, which he shared with other German romanticists, together with his weakness for preconceived notions, was too strong.

CONCLUSIONS

The influence of Tieck on America was various and extensive. Tieck attracted the attention of the 'Göttingen men:' George Bancroft, Henry Edwin Dwight, and George Ticknor. The latter saw him frequently during his extended visit to Dresden from November, 1835, to May 12, 1836, as well as during a later visit, and Tieck's contacts with him were more significant than with any other American whom he met. He was also visited by Motley, and there were shorter personal contacts with the following Americans: Edward Robinson, probably his wife, Therese von Jacob, Francis Lieber, and Walter Haven. Most of these contacts occurred during Tieck's Dresden period. Bancroft, though familiar with Tieck's *Minnelieder*, his romantic writings such as *Genoveva*, his proposed Shakespeare translation, and his translation of *Don Quixote*, gave him but grudging recognition as a poet and writer, very likely because of an anti-romantic bias. The other Americans who had significant contacts with Tieck, such as Ticknor, Dwight, and Motley, were more favorably disposed toward him. Their interest in Tieck stemmed from his brilliant readings of Shakespearean plays, for which he had been noted in Dresden, his Shakespeare enthusiasm, and various Shakespeare projects. Motley admired the writings of Tieck's romantic period, as evidenced in a translation of *The Blue Beard*. Ticknor extended his Shakespearean interest to include early English literature in general, and shared with Tieck an interest in early Spanish literature, the study of Dante, and admiration of Goethe.

Karl Follen stimulated an interest in German literature in Cambridge and Boston by his inspiring work as teacher at Harvard and by the compilation of one of the earliest and most influential German readers and grammars. His inaugural address elicited a very enthusiastic reply from John Quincy Adams. He inspired Margaret Fuller and others at Cambridge to deepen their study of German. He was evidently an admirer of Tieck. He included large selections from him in his reader and mentioned him in his inaugural address among the highest names of modern German literature. In his letter to John Quincy Adams, he placed him at the head of the romantic school, praising, in his *Phantasus*, his typically German, mystical spirit and his successful struggle against sickly sentimentality. Because of his great influence as a teacher, his admiration helped to contribute to a favorable interest in Tieck. Brooks, who had been a student of Follen's at Harvard, used the selection of Tieck's "Frühling" which Follen had included in his *Lesebuch* as the basis for his English translation of that poem, and this in turn was included by Longfellow in his *Poets and Poetry of Europe*. Follen may also have induced Margaret Fuller to study Tieck, since he was one of the three persons who had the strongest influence upon her German studies. James Freeman Clarke, who also influenced her, was himself a devoted reader of Tieck.

Chapters Two and Three show the popularity which Tieck enjoyed in the American literary world in the nineteenth century. Really significant interest in Tieck does not begin until the twenties, but a short statistical survey shows that up to the end of the fifties—the decade of Tieck's death—there were thirty general articles as compared to eight to the end of the nineteenth century and sixteen translations as compared to five after that period. At the same time the number of school editions, German reprints, treatments in histories of German literature, and the like were equal in number—eight each. This would seem to show that the general cultural interest in Tieck dropped after the fifties and that after that date it became scholarly and academic. This parallels the situation in England, where, according to Zeydel, the change in appreciation of Tieck occurred in the fifties, "the later period" disclosing "more cool criticism than the earlier." In Germany, according to Hewett-Thayer, the change came about in the thirties. This change is due to the trend toward realism which reacted against Tieck, generally regarded as a romantic writer. There is an anti-romantic trend in the Tieck criticism of the latter half of the century, as may be seen in the reprints of 1853 from the *Athenaeum*, of 1854 from the *British Quarterly Review*, in the important articles by Boyesen in *The Atlantic Monthly* (1875, 1876), and in the histories of German literature by Hosmer (1879), Francke (1896f.), and Wells (1897).

England shows considerable influence in these articles and translations. Five or six articles and four translations are reprints from English journals. (Whether the *Tribune* was a British magazine or not could not be determined.) The influence of Carlyle is noticeable, there being two reprints from his translations of Tieck, one of them without acknowledgement.

Chapter Four, "Tieck and American Authors," shows that Tieck influenced numerous American writers, but that his effect was not to enslave the American author to the foreign influence. This is to be expected, for the more creative the personality of an author, the less does he merely imitate. He tends rather to assimilate and re-digest in his own terms. This may be seen in the three American authors whom Tieck influenced most: Irving, Longfellow, and Hawthorne. Irving met Tieck and read and admired some of his works, particularly the tales of his earlier period. He was indebted to Tieck for the device of the framed tale in his *Tales of a Traveller*, the technique used by Tieck in his *Phantasus* (although Irving had used this technique in *Bracebridge Hall*, and the club Fancy is far removed from the spirit of the cultured circle in *Phantasus*). There are also some resemblances between *The Bold Dragoon* and Tieck's *Vogelscheuche*. Irving absorbed from Tieck the enthusiasm of the German romanticists for the Spanish past. Tieck's influence helped to confirm the tendencies which Irving already possessed and had developed independently.

Longfellow was well acquainted with the early phase of Tieck's literary production. He mentions him in *Hyperion* and in his journals. He also owned a number of works by Tieck and inserted a notice on Tieck in his *Poets and Poetry of Europe*. Tieck's influence on his creative writing was confined to his poetry, since he had but little respect for Tieck's prose. In *Hyperion*, he considered him and Uhland, "the best living poets of Germany," and from him he derived in part his antiquarianism, mediaevalism, and romantic lyrical mood.

The relation between Tieck and other American authors was either transitional, as with Margaret Fuller, anecdotal, as with Cooper, or incidental, as with Emerson, Thoreau, Lowell, and Fitz James O'Brien.

Poe knew enough of Tieck's *Journey into the Blue Distance* in the original to understand the title and something of its richly imaginative content, so that he was able to enhance the fantastic atmosphere of his *Fall of the House of Usher*. Most of his knowledge was derived at third-hand through American and British magazines. Poe was not admitted to Hawthorne's workshop and knew only his finished products. From a reprint in *The Democratic Review* for April, 1845, on "American Humor" he learned of some similarity between Hawthorne and Tieck. He confirmed his notion of Tieck from what he read in earlier British reviews and from an English translation of Tieck's *Die Freunde* in an American journal. With this limited knowledge, he could state that Tieck's manner "in *some* of his works, is absolutely identical with that *habitual* to Hawthorne." Hawthorne's narrative writing resembles that of Tieck in motivation though not in style. The resemblance in motivation is general, such as one is likely to find "in the air" during a period when the influence of English and German romanticism was dominant. The relationship between *Feathertop* and Tieck's *Vogelscheuche*, however, is definite. But the influence is of Tieck's tale on the Note of 1849, one of the steps in Hawthorne's evolution of his story, rather than on the finished product itself, and of content rather than style.

Chapter Six shows that Tieck's reaction to America was negative. Tieck, like other German romanticists, disliked contemporary America for its philistinism and lack of intellectual tradition. Despite his unfavorable attitude, there can be no doubt that his interest in its literature, geography, and history was very considerable, as shown by his library holdings.

While it does not come within the limits of this study, Tieck's importance in the twentieth century is definitely established in American academic circles. Will this regard for Tieck spread to the American cultivated public in general as it did between the second and fifth decades of the nineteenth century? This would depend on whether there is a general revival of interest in German romanticism. There are several trends in literature and science today which would lead one to consider this a possibility. Tieck's nature demonism as seen in his *Der blonde Eckbert* and *Der Runenberg* is similar to the interest in the subconscious developed by Joyce and Eliot. The devices used by Tieck in his fantastic comedies, like *Der gestiefelte Kater*, were reapplied by Wilder in his *Skin of our Teeth*. Tieck's striving for totality of experience seems to foreshadow Einstein's hypothesis, which attempts to bring together both the magnetic and gravitational systems in one unity. It is, of course, dangerous to prophesy. But should these various trends unite, it is by no means inconceivable that we might again have a general revival of interest in German romanticism in America which would carry with it a general revival of interest in Tieck as well.

APPENDIX

A List of American Books in Tieck's Library
According to the Asher Catalog of 1849

The first number is a reference to the page where the item occurs in the Asher Catalog; the second, to its number. For obvious reasons reprints of editions by English authors which appeared in the United States, have not been included.

In view of the great size of the second section (Books dealing with the History, Geography, Travels etc., of North and South America) which runs from page 196 to 211 in the Asher Catalog and includes 266 items, we made a selective bibliography, choosing only such items as appeared of striking importance to us with special emphasis on North America with which we are chiefly concerned in this study.

Catalogue de la Bibliothèque Célèbre de M. Ludwig Tieck Qui Sera Vendue A Berlin Le 10. Décembre 1849 Et Jours Suivants Par Mm. A Asher & Comp. Berlin, 1849.

I. American Language and Literature

Page No.
65 1624. Allston, Wash. Monaldi. Eine Erzählung. Deutsch v. Kahldorff. 8 vo. Leipzig 1843. cart.
66 1643. Bartlett, J. R. Dictionary of Americanism. A glossary of words and phrases usually regarded as peculiar to the United States. 8 vo. New-York 1848. cart. à l'angl.
68 1675. Bryant, W. C. Poems, with illustr. by F. Leutze, engraved by American artists. gr. in 8 vo. Philadelphia 1847. cart. a l'angl. tr. dor.
69 1709. Channing, Wil. E. Self-culture. 8 vo. Boston 1839. br.
70 1745. Cooper, J. F. The Headsman. 8 vo. Paris 1833. d.r.
    1746. ——— ——— Lionel Lincoln. 3 vols. 8 vo. London 1824. cart. n.r.
    1747. ——— ——— The last of the Mohikans. 3 vols. 8 vo. Ib. 1824. cart. n.r.
    1748. ——— ——— The Pilot. 3 vols. 8 vo. Ib. 1824. cart. n.r.
    1749. ——— ——— Autre édition. 3 vols. 8 vo. Paris 1825. d.r.
    1750. ——— ——— The Prairie. 3 vols. 8 vo. London 1827. cart. n.r.
    1751. ——— ——— The Pioneers. 3 vols. 8 vo. Ib. 1824. cart. n.r.
    1752. ——— ——— The Spy. 3 vols. 8 vo. Ib 1823. cart. n.r.
    1753. ——— ——— Autre édition. 3 vols. en 1. 8 vo. Leipzig 1825. d.r.
75 1878. (Halliburton.) The Bubbles of Canada. By the author of "Sam Slick" etc. 8 vo. Philadelphia 1839. cart. à l'angl.

	1879.	—— —— Autre édition. 8 vo. London 1839. cart. n.r.

1879. —— —— Autre édition. 8 vo. London 1839. cart. n.r.

1880. —— —— The Clockmaker; or sayings and doings of Sam. Slick. 8 vo. Philadelphia 1837. cart. à l'angl.

1881. —— —— 2d series. 8 vo. Philadelphia 1838. cart.

76 1897. Hoffmann, C. F. Greyslaer; a romance of the Mohawk. 3 vols. 8 vo. London 1840. cart. n.r.

1920. Irving, Wash. Works, with a memoir of the author. gr. in 8 vo. Paris 1831. d.r.

1921. —— —— Autre édition. gr. in 8 vo. Francfort o.M. 1835 d.r.

77 1922. Irving, Wash. The Alhambra. 2 vols. 12 mo. Paris 1834. br. n.r.

1923. —— —— A chronicle of the conquest of Granada. 2 vols. 8 vo. London 1829. d.r.

1924. —— —— The Sketch-book. 2 vols. 8 vo. London 1824. cart. n.r.

1925. —— —— Autre édition. 2 vols en 1. 12 mo. Paris 1834. d.r.

1926. —— —— Jonathan Oldstyles Briefe. Deutsch. v. S. H. Spiker. 8 vo. Berlin 1824. br.

1930. [1]Jones, George. Tecumseh, tragedy.—Biography of general Harrison.—Oration upon life, character and genius of Shakspeare. gr. en 8 vo. London 1844. cart. à l'angl.

90 2263. Sigourney, Mrs. Sketches. 8 vo. Philadelphia 1834. cart. à l'angl.

94 2346. Webster, Noah. An American dictionary of the English language, first edition in Octavo, containing the whole vocabulary of the Quarto, with corrections, improvements and several thousand additional words. 2 vols. Impérial 8 vo. New Haven 1841. cart. à l'angl.

II. Books dealing with the History, Geography, Travels etc., of North and South America

196 4382. Achenwall, D. G. Einige Anmerkungen über Nord-Amerika und über dasige Grossbritannische Colonien. 8 vo. Helmstedt 1777. br.

4383. Acosta, Joseph de. Historia natural y moral de las Indias. 4 to. Sevilla 1590. veau. marbre. *Première édition; très rare.*

4384. —— —— Ontdekking van West-Indien, vlijtig ondersogt, en naauvkeurig aangeteekend 1592 en vervolgens. fig. 8 vo. Leyden 1706. br.

---

[1] This author, George Jones, 1810-1879, who later acquired the title Count Johannes, presents an interesting problem in regard to nationality. He was born an Englishman but came early to America, where he was active as an actor and writer, as well as a lawyer. Since, however, there seems to be no absolutely clear evidence that he ever became a citizen, we leave it to the reader to determine his nationality.

4385. Acrelius, Israel. Beskrifning om de Svenska Försammlingars tillstand uti America. 4to. Stockholm 1759.
4386. Amerikanerin, die junge, oder Verkürzung müssiger Stunden auf dem Meere. 4 part. en 2 vols. 8 vo. Ulm 1765-68. br. n.r.
4390. Anmerkenswaardigeen zeldzame West-Indische Zee en Land-Reizen, door de Caraibische Eylanden, Nieuw-Nederland, Virginien, en de Spaansche West-Indien. fig. 4to. Amsterdam 1705. vel.
4391. Antiquitates Americanae sive scriptores septentrionales rerum ante-Columbianarum in America. *Grand papier.* fig. et cart. 4to. Hafniae 1837. d. r.
4395. Baqueville de la Potherie. Histoire de l'Amérique septentrionale. fig. 4 vol. 8 vo. Paris 1722. br. non rogné. *Rare.*
197 4417. Bordone, Benedetto. Libro di B. B., nel qual si ragiona de tutte e' Isole del mondo con li lor nomi antichi e moderni, historie, favole, e modi del loro vivere e in qual parte del mare stanno e in qual parallelo e clima giacciono. fol. s.l. (Venetiae?) 1528. d. r. *Fig. en bois. Première édition, très rare. Cet ouvrage contient des Cartes de Cuba, Jamaica, du Coté de Labrador etc.*
198 4418. Bouchette, J. A topographical dictionary of the province of Lower Canada. 4to. London 1832. cart. a l'angl.
4419. Boyer, P. Véritable relation de tout ce qui s'est fait et passé au voyage que M. de Brétigny fit en l'Amérique-Occidentale, avec une description des moeurs et des provinces de tous les sauvages de cette grande partie du cap Nord: un dictionnaire de la langue Galibienne etc. etc. 8 vo. Paris 1654. veau.
198 4423. Büttner, der Amerikaner. Eine Selbstbiographie Joh. Carl Büttners. 2te Aufl. Portr. 8 vo. Camenz 1828. d. r.
4424. Californie. Histoire naturelle et civile de la Californie, trad. de l'Angl. 3 vols. 8 vo. Paris 1767. cart.
4425. Natürl. u. bürgerl. Geschichte von Californien, nebst einer Karte. Aus d. Engl. von J. C. Adelung. 3 part en 1. vol. 4to. Lemgo 1769. veau. d.r.
4426. Campanius, Thom. Beskrifning om Provincien Nye Sverige uti America. 4to. Stockholm 1702.
4432. Charlevoix, de. Histoire et description generale de la Nouvelle-France avec le journal historique d'un voyage fait par ordre du Roi dans l'Amérique septentrionale. Cartes. 3 vols. 4to. Paris 1744. veau.
4433. C (lodoré), J. Relation de ce qui s'est passé dans les Isles et terre-ferme de l'Amérique, pendant la dernière guerre avec l'Angleterre, et depuis en execution du Traitté de Breda avec un journal du dernier voyage du Sr. de la Barre en la Terre-ferme etc. 2 vols. 8 vo. Paris 1671. veau. *Rare.*
199 4435. Colombo, Fernand. Historie nelle quali s'ha particolare e vera relatione della vita et de fatti del'Ammiraglio D. Christoforo Colombo, suo padre et dello scropimento ch'egli fece dell' Indie Occidentali, dette Mondo Nuovo. 8 vo. Venetia 1571. d.r. *Première édition; Rare.*

199	4442.	*Cosmographiae* introductio cum quisbusdam geometriae ac astronomiae principiis ad eam rem necessariis. Insuper quatuor **A m e r i c i V e s p u c i j** navigationes. Universalis chosmographiae descriptio tam in solido, quam in plano, eis etiam insertis que in Phtolomeo ignota a nuperis reperta sunt. Fig. d'Astronomie. 4to. Deodatae 1507. (In fine) : Finutu. iiij. kl' Septebris Anno supra sesquimillesimu. vij. br. *Ouvrage de la plus grande importance pour l'histoire de la découverte de l'Amérique, importance suffisamment reconnue par M. de Humboldt (Kosmos II. 490.) Mais ce que donne au présent exemplaire une importance additionelle, c'est ce qu'il est d'une édition entièrement inconnue aux Bibliographes, qui ne citent que la seule du VII. May 1507. Notre édition, datée du IV. Sept. de la même année prouve le grand succès qu'avait ce livre. L'exempl. est d'une conservation parfaite.*
	4445.	Davila, Gil Gonzales, et Fern. Cortes. Twee onderscheydene Reys-togten d'eene ter Zee en d'andere te Land, in de West-Indien, beyde gedaan in het Jaar 1524. cart. et fig. 8 vo. Leyden 1706. br.
200	4449.	Denys. Geographische en historische beschrijving der Kusten van Noord-America, met de Natuurlijke Historie des Landts. fig. 4to. Amsterdam 1688. br.
	4454.	Dunn, John. History of the Oregon territory. Carte. 8 vo. London 1846. cart. à l'angl.
	4456.	Ebeling, Chr. D. Erdbeschreibung und Geschichte von Amerika. 5 vols. 8 vo. Hamburg 1793-1799. d.r.
	4458.	Elogj storici di Cristoforo Colombo e di Andrea D'Oria. 4to. Parma, Bodoni. 1781. vel.
	4462.	Feuillet, Le R.P. Journal des observations phisiques, mathematiques et botaniques en Amérique. 3 part. en 2 vols. fig. cartes. 4to. Paris 1714-25.
200	4463.	Franciscus, Erasm. Neu-polirter Geschicht-Kunst-und Sittenspiegel ausländischer Voelker: der Sineser, Japaner, Indostaner, Mexicaner, Brasilianer etc. etc. fig. fol. Nürnberg 1670. veau.
	4464.	Fremont, J. C. Narrative of the exploring expedition to the Rocky mountains in 1842, and to Oregon and North-California in 1843. 44. fig. carte. 8 vo. London 1846. cart. à l'angl.
201	4470.	(Garcilasso de la Vega.) Geschichte der Eroberung v. Florida, deutsch v. H. L. Meyer. 8 vo. Zelle. Frankf. u. Leipz. 1753. cart. n.r.
	4474.	Gottfriedt, Joh. Ludw. Newe Welt u. Amerikan. Historien innhaltende Beschreibung aller West-Indianischen Landschaften, Insuln etc. fig. et cartes par Merian. fol. Frankf. a.M. 1631. veau.
	4475.	——— ——— Autre édition. fig. fol. Franckfurt 1655. r.d.t. *Exempl. raccommodé.*
201	4476.	Gray, Fr. C. Prison discipline in America. 8 vo. London 1848. br. n.r.

4480. Happelius, E. G. Mundus mirabilis tripartitus oder Wunderbare Welt in einer kurtzen Cosmographia. fig. 3 vols. 4to. Ulm 1687. vel. *Ces ouvrages curieux contiennent un grand nombre de notices géographiques, historiques etc. sur l'Amérique.*

4481. —— —— Denkwürdigkeiten der Welt. fig. 4 vols. 4to. Hamburg 1683-89. veau.

202 4482. Happelius, E. G. Thesaurus exoticorum. Fürstellend die Asiatische, Africanische und Amerikanische Nationes etc. etc. fol. Hamburg 1690.

4485. Hartmann, J. A. Disputatio geographica de vero Californiae situ et conditione. Carte. 8 vo. Marburg. s.d. (1739) br.

4486. Hennepin, L. de Nouvelle Decouverte d'un très grand pays situé dans l'Amerique entre le nouveau Mexique et la Mer Glaciale. fig. et cartes. 12 mo. Utrecht, Bröedelet. 1697. veau. *Première édition de cette partie. Rare.*

4487. —— —— A new discovery of a vast Country in America—with a continuation, to which is added: Several new Discoveries in North America. 8 vo. London 1698. veau.

202 4490. (Herrera, Anton. de.) Description de las Indias Occidentales. 8 decades en 5 vols. fig. et cartes. fol. Madrid 1730. vel. *Édition de la plus complète de cet ouvrage célèbre.*

4491. —— —— Aankomst van Jean d'Ezquebel ter Bevolking van Jamaica, door den Ammiraal Diego Kolumbus van Hispaniola derwaards gezonden, in't Jaar 1510. fig. 8 vo. Leyden 1706. br.

4495. Hesselius, Andreas. Om de Svenska Kyrkans nu varande Tillstand i America. 4to. Norköping 1725.

4497. Hilliard d'Aubreteuil. Essais historiques et politiques sur les Anglo-Americains. fig. 2 vols. 8 vo. Brux. 1781. r.d.s.t.

4498. Hinton, J. H. The history and topography of the United States, illustrated with a series of views, drawn on the spot and engraved on steel. 2 vols. gr. 4to. London 1830. cart. à l'angl.

203 4500. Hitchcock, E. Report on the geology, mineralogy, botany and zoology of Massachusetts. 8 vo. et Atlas in fol. fig. Amsterdam 1835. cart. à l'angl.

4501. Hughes, Griffith. The natural history of Barbados. 29 fig. fol. London 1750. veau.

4503. Inga, Ath. West-Indische Spieghel, waerinne men sien kan, alle de Eylanden . . . , het mächtige Ryck van Mexico en't gout en silver-rycke Landt van Peru. fig. et cart. 4to. Amsterdam 1624. vel.

4504. Jamaica. Ste State of the Island of Jamaica, chiefly in Relation to its commerce and the conduct of the Spaniards in the West-Indies. London 1725.—Some Observations on the Assiento Trade proving the Damage, which will accrue thereby to the British Commerce and Plantations in America and particularly to Jamaica. London 1728.—An Answer to a Calumy with some Remarks upon an anonimous Pamphlet: Some observat. on the

Assiento Trade etc." London 1728.—A Defense of the observations on the Assiento Trade etc. 8 vo. London. veau. *Quatre pièces très rares en un vol.*

4505. Jones, G. History of Ancient America, anterior to the time of Columbus. 8 vo. London 1843. Cart. à l'angl.

4510. (Lafitau, Jos. Fr.) Moeurs des sauvages américains, comparées aux moeurs des premiers temps. 2 vols. 4to. fig. Paris 1724. veau.

4511. Lahontan, Bar de. Voyages dans l'Amérique septentrionale. fig. 2 vols. 8 vo. Amsterdam 1728. br.

4515. Le Blanc, Vincent. Les Voyages fameux du V.L., qu'il a faits aux Indes Orientales et Occidentales etc. etc., redigez par P. Bergeron et corrigé par Coulon. 3 parties en 1 vol. 4to. Paris 1658 v. br. *Ouvrage important, aussi bien pour la connaissance de l'Asie que de l'Amérique. Les chapitres sur le Canada, la Virginie, la Floride etc. sont fort interessants.*

4516. L(eibnitz), G. G. Codex juris gentium diplomaticus cum Mantissa. 2 parties en un vol. fol. Hanoverae 1693-1700. veau. *Parmi les Documens recueillies par le célèbre Leibnitz il y a la lettre de Ferdinand Roi de Sicile à Louis XI et la reponse du dernier, par lesquelles il est prouvé que Christophe Colomb faisait le métier de Corsaire en 1474.—On y trouve aussi la célèbre Bulle du Pape Alexandre VI (du 4. Mai 1493) par laquelle il accorda à Ferdinand et Isabelle le droit de Possession des découvertes de Colomb au deça d'un certain meridien.*

4517. Leiste, Ch. Beschreibung des Brittischen Amerika zur Ersparung der englischen Karten. Nebst einer Special-Karte der mittlern Brittischen Colonien. 8 vo. Wolfenb. 1778.

4519. Leon, J. Ponze de, et Pamphilio de Narvaes. Verscheide Zee en Land-togten gedaan in de West-Indien, Florida etc. in't Jahr 1512 en 1515. cart. et fig. 8 vo. Leyden 1706. br.

4520. Le Page du Pratz. Histoire de la Louisiane; ornée de deux cartes et de 40 planches en taille douce. 3 vol. 8 vo. Paris 1758. veau.

4523. Le Sage. Les avantures de Mr. Robert Chevalier, dit de Beauchène, capitaine de Flibustiers dans la nouv. France. 2 part en 1 vol. fig. 8 vo. Amsterdam 1733. cart.

3050. Lescarbot, Marc. Les Muses de la Nouvelle France. 8 vo. Paris 1618. cart. *Petit volume d'une rareté extrême, qui contient une représentation théâtrale sous le titre Le Théâtre de Neptune en la Nouvelle France representé sur les flots du Port Royal le 14 Novemb. 1606 au retour du Sieur du Poutrincourt du pays des Armouchiquois.*

4524. Lettres édifiantes écrites par quelques Missionnaires de la C. J. de l'Amérique Septentrionale. 8 vo. Bruxelles 1771. veau.

4527. Long, J. Voyages and travels of an Indian interpreter and trader, describing the manners and customs of the North-American Indians. With a vocabulary of the Chippeway language. 4to. London 1791. d.r.

APPENDIX

- 4528. Ludewig, H. E. The litterature of American local history. 8 vo. New-York 1846. cart. à l'angl.
- 4532. M .... Journal d'un voyage à la Louisiane fait en 1720. 8 vo. A la Haye 1768. br.
- 4533. Maffei, J. P. Historiarum Indicarum libri XVI. Accessit Ignatii Lojolae vita. Carte. fol. Coloniae 1593. vel.
- 205 4534. Marquard, Joh. Tractatus politico-juridicus de jure mercatorum et commerciorum singulari. fol. Francofurti 1662. vel. *Ce volume contient toutes les pièces historiques relativement à l'établissement de la Colonie Suédoise en Amérique.*
- 4535. Marquette, P., en Joliet. Ontdekking van eenige landen en volkeren, in't noorder-gedeelte van America in het Jaar 1673. fig. 8 vo. Leyden 1707. br.
- 4537. Martin, Rob. Montg. History of the Colonies of the British Empire in the West Indies, South America, North America, Asia etc. and Europe. Carte. gr. in 8 vo. à 2 col. London 1843. cart. à l'angl.
- 4540. Mémoires historiques sur la Louisiane, depuis l'année 1687 jusqu'à présent; avec l'établissement de la colonie Française dans cette province. fig. et cartes. 2 vols. 8 vo. s.l. 1753. veau.
- 4543. Montanus, Arnold. De nieuwe en onbekende Weereld, of Beschryving van America en't Zuidland. fig. fol. Amsterdam, Meurs, 1671. veau. *Bel exemplaire.*
- 4544. Moreau de St. Mery. Lois et Constitutions des Colonies de l'Amerique sous le vent. 6 vols. 4to. Paris 1784. veau. *Rare.*
- 205 4546. Münster. Seb. Cosmographiae universalis libri VI. fig. et cart. fol. Basileae 1550 r.d.t.
- 4547. ——— ——— Autre édition. fol. s.l. 1552. d.r.
- 4548. ——— ——— Autre édition. fig. en bois. fol. Basileae 1559. r.d.t.
- 4549. ——— ——— Cosmographei, oder Beschreibung aller Länder, Herrschaften, stetten, geschichten, gebreuche etc. fig. e.b. fol. Basel, H. Petri. 1561. r.d.t. *Édition inconnue à Brunet et Ebert.*
- 4550. ——— ——— Autre édition fig. 3 part. fol. Basel 1628. veau.
- 4551. Neal, Daniel. History of New-England. Carte. 2 vols. 8 vo. London 1720. d.r.
- 206 4563. Pensylvania. An Historical Review of the constitution and government of Pensylvania from its Origin. 8 vo. London 1759. veau.
- 207 4571. Pizarro y Orllana, D. Fr. Varones ilustres del nuevo mundo, describriadores, conquistadores, y pacificadores de las Indias occidentales. fol. Madrid, Diego Diay de la Carrera. 1639. veau. *Ce volume contient les vies de C. Colomb, F. Cortez, les quatre Pizarre, Almagro et Diego Garcia de Paredes.*
- 4572. Pontius, Ribald, Laudonniere, Gourgues en andere. Verscheyde Scheeps-Togten na Florida: gedaan in het Jaar 1562 en vervolgens. fig. 8 vo. Leyden 1706. br.

APPENDIX

4575. Prescott, W. H. History of the reign of Ferdinand and Isabella, the Catholic. 3 vols. 8 vo. Boston 1838. cart. à l'angl.
4576. Priest, William. Travels in the United States of America (1793-97.) Avec une vign. col. 8 vo. London 1802. dem. rel.
4584. Ramsay, David. History of the revolution of South Carolina. 2 vols. 8 vo. Trenton 1785. dem. rel.

208   4587. Reed, A. and J. Matheson. A narrative of the visit to the American churches by the deputation from the Congregational Union of England and Wales. 2 vols. 8 vo. London 1836. cart. à l'angl.

4590. Riedesel, Generalin von. Die Berufs-Reise nach America, Briefe auf dieser Reise und während ihres sechsjährigen Aufenthalts in America zur Zeit des dortigen Krieges in den Jahren 1776-83 nach Deutschland geschrieben. 8 vo. Berlin 1801. br.
4592. Robertson, Will. History of America. 2 vols. 4to. London 1777 d.r.
4593. —— —— Autre édition. 4 vols. 8 vo. London 1803. veau.
4601. Sanson d'Abbeville. L'Amerique en plusieurs cartes nouvelles et exactes et en divers traictes de geographie et d'histoire. cart. 4to. Paris 1662. veau.

209   4606. Scherer, H. Atlas Marianus sive pracipue totius orbis habitati imagines et statuae magnae dei matris beneficiis ac prodigiis inclytae succincta historia propositae et mappis geographicis expressae cartes. 4to. Monachii 1702. br. *Volume fort intéressant qui contient la description de tous les lieux de l'Amérique, de l'Europe et de l'Asie ou l'on pratique l'adoration de la Vierge.*

4607. —— —— Geographia Hierarchica sive status ecclesiastici Romano-Catholici per orbem universum distributi succincta descriptio historico-geographica partes. 4to. Monachii 1703. br. *Ouvrage fort intéressant qui contient la description de tous les lieux de l'Amérique, de l'Europe et de l'Asie ou se trouvent des établissemens de l'Eglise Catholique.*
4610. Sloane, Hans. Voyage to the Islands; Madeira, Barbados Nieves, S. Christophers and Jamaica, with the Natural History . . . . of the last of those Islands, to which is prefix'd an introduction, wherein is an account of the Inhabitants, Air, Waters, Diseases, Trade etc. fig. et cart. 2 vols. folio. London 1707-25. mar. r.tr. dorée.
4611. Smith, John. General History of Virginia, New-England and the Summer Isles with the names of the Adventurers, Planters and Governours from 1584-1626. fol. London 1632. br. *Sans les fig.; titre raccommodé.*

210   4619. Solorzano, Pereira, Joan de. Disquisitiones de Indiarum jure sive de justa Indiarum occidentalium inquisitione, acquisitione, et retentione. 2 part. en 1 vol. Lugduni 1672. r.d.t.

	4620.	———— ———— Politica Indiana, dividida en seis libros. fol. Amberes 1703. veau.
	4621.	Soto, Ferd. de. De gedenkwaardige voyagie na Florida, gedaan anno 1539 en vervolgens. fig. et carte. 8 vo. Leyden 1706. br.
	4624.	Ternaux-Compans, H. Voyages, Relations et Mémoires originaux pour servir à l'histoire de la découverte de l'Amérique. 20 vol. 8 vo. Paris 1840-42. br.
	4625.	Testament, le nouveau, en langue Chippeway. 8 vo. Albany 1833.
	4626.	Thatcher, B. B. Indian Biography, or an historical account of distinguished North American Natives. fig. 2 vols. 12 mo. New-York 1832. cart. en perc.
	4633.	Touron. Histoire générale de l'Amérique depuis sa découverte. 14 vols. 8 vo. Paris 1768-70. br.
	4634.	Tucker, G. Progress of the United States in population and wealth. 8 vo. New-York 1843. cart. à l'angl.
	4638.	Ulloa, D. Jorge Juan et D. Ant. de. Noticias Americanas. Entretenimientos fisico-históricos sobre la América meridional y la septentrional-oriental: Comparacion general de los Territorios Climas y Producciones en las tres especies Vegetal, Animal y Mineral etc. 4to. Madrid 1792. d.r.
	4639.	———— ———— Mémoires philosophiques, historiques, physiques, concernant la découverte de l'Amérique. Traduit par M. * * * 2 vols. 8 vo. Paris 1787. cart. à l'angl.
211	4640.	V., S. v. Ausführliche Beschreibung des theils bewohnt-teils unbewohnt-sogenannten Grönlands. Durch S. von V. Cartes. 4to. Nürnberg 1679. br.
211	4642.	Vaugondy, de. Mémoire sur les pays de l'Asie et de l'Amérique situés au nord de la mer de sud: accompagné d'une Carte. 4to. Paris 1774. br. *Rare*.
	4643.	Verhandeling over de Nederlandsche Ontdekkingen in Amerika, Australië, de Indiën en de Poollanden. Uitgegeven door het Provinciaal Utrechtsche Genootschap. 8 vo. Utrecht 1827. br.
	4645.	Villagutierrez de Soto Mayor, Juan de. Historia de la provincia de el Ilza, reduccion y progresos de el Lacandon y otras naciones de Indios barbaros de la mediacion de el reyne de Guatimala a las provincias de Yucatan en la America septentrional. fol. Madrid 1701. c.d.R.
	4646.	Vries, S. de. Curieuse Aenmerkingen der bysonderste Oost en West-Indische verwonderenswaerdige Dingen. fig. part. 1 et 2. 4to. Utrecht 1682. vel.
	4647.	Weld, Isaac. Travels through the States of North America etc.; Upper and Lower Canada during the years 1795-97. fig. 8 vo. London 1800. veau.
	4648.	Zorgdrager, C. G. Bloeijende Opkomst der Aloude en Hedendaagsche Groenlandsche Visschery, uitgebreid door Abraham Moubach. fig. et cartes. 4to. Amsterdam 1728 vel. *L'édition hollandaise de cet ouvrage célèbre est la plus complète et la*

plus estimée; les additions qu'elle contient sont d'une grande importance.

III. Miscellaneous. Theology, Philosophy, Archeology, etc.

330	7231.	Buxton, Th. F. Der afrikanische Sklavenhandel. Deutsch von G. Julius. Mit einer Vorr.: Die Niegerexpedition und ihre Bestimmung v.C. Ritter. 8 vo. Leipzig 1841. cart.
334	7315.	Esclavage. The south vindicated from the treason and fanaticism of the northern abolitionists. 8 vo. Philadelphia 1836. cart.
	7316.	—— —— Slavery in America; being a review of Miss Martineau on that subject, by a South Carolinian. 8 vo. Richmond 1838. br.
347	7614.	Paulding, J. K. Slavery in the United States. 8 vo. New-York 1836. cart.

IV. Books Omitted

359	7872.	Ebeling's, Chr. D. Erdbeschreibung und Geschichte von Amerika. 5 vols. 8 vo. Hamburg 1793-99. d.r.

BIBLIOGRAPHY[1]

I. Works by Tieck, and Wackenroder; and American and English Authors

A. Works by Tieck and Wackenroder

(a) In German

Musen-Almanach für das Jahr 1802, herausgegeben von A. W. Schlegel und L. Tieck. Tübingen, 1802.

Ludwig Tieck's sämmtliche Werke. Wien, 1817-1824. 30 v. (a pirated edition of Tieck's works).

Follen, Charles. *Deutsches Lesebuch für Anfänger.* Cambridge, 1826, 149-75 (Contains *Der blonde Eckbert* and the poem, "Die Lilie. Romanze." 239-41. Later editions beginning with the second, Boston, 1831 edition, substituted selections from the *Blaubart* and *Der gestiefelte Kater* respectively for *Der blonde Eckbert,* and for the poem "Lilie," the poems "Frühling" and "Der Verschmähte" (*ibid.*, 155-89, 239-40). From the Boston, 1836 edition on, the *Blaubart* selections occur on pp. 116-23, the selections from *Der gestiefelte Kater* on pp. 124-54, the two poems "Frühling" and "Der Verschmähte" on pages 199 and 199-200 respectively. The 1858 edition which was brought out by G. A. Schmitt after Follen's death, contains only the two poems listed above).

Ludwig Tieck's Schriften. Berlin, 1828-1854. 28v. This edition is referred to as *Schriften* in the text.

Bokum, Herman. *An Introduction to the Study of the German Language* Comprising Extracts from the Best German Prose Writers, with an English Interlinear Translation, Explanatory Notes, and a Treatise on Pronunciation, Affording the Means of a Ready and Accurate Comparison of the Idioms of the Two Languages ... Second Edition, Corrected and Improved. Philadelphia, 1832. The German 'literal' text and the English literal and free interlinear translation occur pages 116 to 139, the standard German text on pages 183 to 191 of the edition.

Tieck, Ludwig. *Das Zauberschloss.* Novelle von Ludwig Tieck; *Pietro von Abano oder Petrus Apone.* Zaubergeschichte von Ludwig Tieck. New York, 1839, 3-84; 3-70.

Briefe an Ludwig Tieck, ausgewählt und herausgegeben von Karl von Holtei. Breslau, 1864. 4 v., especially III, 353; IV, 104.

Kritische Schriften, zum erstenmale gesammelt und mit einer Vorrede herausgegeben von Ludwig Tieck. Leipzig, 1848-1852. 4 v., especially IV, 355.

Roelker, Bernard. *A German Reader for Beginners.* Second Revised and

---

[1]The author will gladly furnish page references upon request. The magazines mentioned in Chapters II and III, on "Tieck's Reception in American Magazines and Books Prior to 1900," and "American Translations of Tieck" respectively, are not repeated, as they are discussed in full in those chapters. Items which are used as reference only once in the entire book are listed by the actual page where the reference occurs.

Improved Edition. Cambridge, 1854. (The poem, "Die Sterne und der Wandersmann," 93-94, *Der blonde Eckbert*, 102-26).
Tieck, L. *Die Elfen, Das Rothkäppchen*. Boston, 1865.
Rosenstengel, W. H. *A Reader of German Literature Prepared for High Schools, Colleges and German-American Schools*. New York and London, 1884. (Reprints with a brief note, Tieck's poem "Zuversicht," 151, 152, 397).
Wackenroder, Wilhelm Heinrich. *Werke und Briefe*. Jena, 1910. 2 v.

(b) In English Translation.[2]

Carlyle, Thomas (ed.)
  German Romance: Specimens of its chief authors, with biographical critical notices, by the translator of Wilhelm Meister, and the author of the Life of Schiller. Edinburgh, London, 1827, II.
  Tales by Musaeus, Tieck, Richter, translated from the German. [Reprinted] New York, 1874, I (1827), 169-85; II (1827), 1-20.
The Pictures in *Foreign Tales and Traditions chiefly selected from the fugitive literature in Germany* (by G. G. Cunningham). 1830.
The Old Man of the Mountain, The Lovecharm, and Pietro of Abano. Tales from the German of Tieck. London, 1831.
Austin, Sarah. *Fragments from German Prose Writers*. London, 1841, 111-20. (Fragments of conversations from *Phantasus*.)
Oxenford, John; Feiling, C. A. *Tales from the German, comprising specimens from the most celebrated authors*. London, 1844. (Contains "The Klausenburg," 231-60.)
Smith, Jane Browning. *The Life and Death of Little Red Ridinghood.* A Tragedy, adapted from the German of Ludwig Tieck. London, 1851, 9 f.
Baskerville, Alfred. *The Poetry of Germany*. New York, 1854. (Contains 163-67 the poems, 'Magelone,' 'Trauer,' 'Herbstlied,' 'Zuversicht.')
Hedge, Frederic H. *Prose Writers of Germany*. Fourth Edition. New York, London, 1856 (contains 498-506, a biographical comment on Tieck and a reprint of *The Elves*).
The Token; a Christmas and New-Years Gift. New York, 1857 (contains 39-103 a translation of Tieck's "The Klausenburg").
Hedge, Frederic Henry. *Hours with German Classics*. Boston, 1886 (pp. 463-473: preface on Tieck's life and a translation of a selection from *Die Denkwürdige Geschichtschronik der Schildbürger*).
Warner, Charles Dudley. *Library of the World's Best Literature Ancient and Modern*. New York, cop. 1897, XXV, 14943-14960 (biographical comment and a reprint of *The Fair-Haired Eckbert*, edited by Professor Willard Fiske).
The Ridpath Library of Universal Literature. New York, 1898, XXIII, no paging.
Francke, Kuno; Howard, William G. *The German Classics of the Nineteenth and Twentieth Centuries*. New York, cop. 1913, IV, 272-93 (reprint of Tieck's *The Elves*).

---

[2] Only books are listed here. Cf. footnote 1.

B. Works by American and English Authors

(Cooper, James Fenimore) *Sketches of Switzerland.* By an American. Part Second. Philadelphia, 1836, I, iii, 7, 198 f.

Emerson, Ralph Waldo:

Norton, Charles Eliot. *The Correspondence of Thomas Carlyle and Ralph Waldo Emerson 1834-1872.* Boston, 1883, I, 266, II, 224.

The Complete Works of Ralph Waldo Emerson, with a Biographical Introduction and Notes, by Edward Waldo Emerson. London, Boston, and New York, (preface March 12, 1904) IX, 249-51, 488-9; (cop. 1893, 1904), XII, 392-404, 481-2.

Journals of Ralph Waldo Emerson, with Annotations edited by Edward Waldo Emerson and Waldo Emerson Forbes. Boston and New York, cop. 1910, 1911, vols. IV, V, VI.

Rusk, Ralph L. *The Letters of Ralph Waldo Emerson.* New York, 1939, III, 98, 116.

Fuller, Margaret:

[Clarke, James Freeman; Emerson, Ralph Waldo; Channing, William Henry] *Memoirs of Margaret Fuller Ossoli.* Boston, MDCCCLII, I, 168 f., 214 f., 241 f.

Hawthorne, Nathaniel:

Letter to Longfellow from Salem, March 21, 1838 (in possession of Longfellow House, Cambridge).

The Works of Nathaniel Hawthorne, with Introductory Notes by George Parsons Lathrop and Nathaniel Hawthorne and his wife; a biography by Julian Hawthorne. (Standard Library Edition). Boston and New York, (cop. 1882-cop. 1896) 15 v.

Passages from The American Note-Books of Nathaniel Hawthorne. Boston and New York, 1890, 211.

Stewart, Randall. *The American Notebooks by Nathaniel Hawthorne,* based upon the Original Manuscripts in the Pierpont Morgan Library. New Haven, cop. 1932. (A comparison with the pertinent passages of the manuscript deposited in the Pierpont Morgan Library of New York has convinced me of the great accuracy of Randall Stewart's reproduction). 176-180, and *passim.*

[Irving, Washington.] Journal 1823 January 10, The First Dresden Diary (N.Y.P.L.); Journal, The Second Dresden Diary, January 20,—May 20, 1823 (N.Y.P.L.).

The Works of Washington Irving. New Edition, Revised. Vol. VII. *Tales of a Traveller* by Geoffrey Crayon, Gent. Author's Revised Edition. New York, 1860.

Trent, William P.; Hellman, George S. *The Journals of Washington Irving* (Hitherto Unpublished). Boston, 1919, I, 155.

Longfellow, Henry Wadsworth. (various pertinent materials available in Longfellow House, Cambridge: Longfellow's Journals 1836 to 1855 *passim*); lecture notes for the year 1837; manuscript material in connection with *The Poets and Poetry of Europe*).

Longfellow, Henry Wadsworth. *The Poets and Poetry of Europe,* with Introductions and Biographical Notices. Philadelphia, 1845, New York and London, 1855, Boston, 1871, vi, 187, 333-34 (333-34 contain a notice on Tieck and two poems, 'Spring,' and 'Song from Bluebeard'; 187 has another reference to Tieck).

The Prose Works of Henry Wadsworth Longfellow. Boston and New York, 1890, II.

Samuel Longfellow. *Life of Henry Wadsworth Longfellow with Extracts from his Journals and Correspondence.* Boston and New York (cop. 1886, 1887, 1891) I, 360, 405; II, 3-4.

Lowell, James Russell. *The Writings of James Russell Lowell.* London, 1900, II, 130 f.; 1894, III, 69 f.; 1893, IX, 1, 60.

O'Brien, Fitz-James. *The Diamond Lens and Other Stories*, with an Introduction by Gilbert Seldes. New York, 1932 (contains "Duke Humphrey's Dinner," 215-38).

Poe, Edgar Allan:
Harrison, James A. *The Complete Works of Edgar Allan Poe.* New York, 1902. 17 v.

Thoreau, Henry David:
The Writings of Henry David Thoreau with Biographical Introductions and Full Indexes. Boston and New York, cop. 1867, 1893; 1863, 1866, 1883, 1893, I, 70, 71; X, 365-429.

II. Other Works Consulted
A. Books

Alterton, Margaret; Craig, Hardin. *Edgar Allan Poe.* Representative Selections, With Introduction, Bibliography, and Notes (*American Writers Series*). New York, Cincinnati, etc., (cop. 1935), 515.

Baginsky, Paul H. *German Works Relating to America 1493-1800.* A List Compiled from the Collections of the New York Public Library, Part X, 1282 (*Bulletin of the New York Public Library*, January, 1940, volume 44) 40.

Bancroft, George:
Notes in MS on Friedrich Bouterwek's course in the history of German literature (Manuscript Division of the New York Public Library) *Literary and Historical Miscellanies.* New York, 1855, 167-205.

Barba, Preston A. *Cooper in Germany.* (*Indiana University Studies.* No. 21, Indiana University Bulletin, 1914, XII, No. 5) 73, 74 f.

Beers, Henry A. *A History of English Romanticism in the Nineteenth Century.* New York, 1910, 162-4.

Biedermann. *Goethes Gespräche*, II, 500-501.

Bouterwek, Friedrich. *Geschichte der Poesie und Beredsamkeit seit dem Ende des dreizehnten Jahrhunderts.* Göttingen, 1812, IX, 95-104; XI, 432-3.

Boyesen, Hjalmar Hjorth. *Essays on German Literature.* New York, 1892. (References to Tieck in the articles, "Social Aspects of the German Romantic School," "Novalis and the Blue Flower," occur 296-330, *passim*; to "Literary Aspects of the Romantic School," 332-44; other references from 345-55, *passim*).

Braun, Frederick Augustus. *Margaret Fuller and Goethe.* The Development of a Remarkable Personality, Her Religion and Philosophy, and

her Relation to Emerson, J. F. Clarke and Transcendentalism. New York, 1910, 41 f.
Brooks, Charles T. *Songs and Ballads*; translated from Uhland, Körner, Bürger, and other German Lyric Poets. With Notes. (*Specimens of Foreign Standard Literature.* Edited by George Ripley. vol. XIV.) Boston, London, 1842, 277.
Brooks, Van Wyck. *The World of Washington Irving.* Philadelphia, 1944, 207, 341.
Calvert, George H. *A Lecture on German Literature*; Being a Sketch of its History from its Origin to the Present Day; Delivered by Request before The Athenaeum Society of Baltimore. Reprinted from the Southern Literary Messenger. Baltimore, 1836, 22.
Cameron, Kenneth Walter. *Ralph Waldo Emerson's Reading.* Raleigh, 1941, 23, 26, 77.
Campbell, Killis. "Poe's Reading." *Studies in English Number 5 (University of Texas Bulletin,* No. 2538) (October 8, 1925), 188.
Canby, Henry Seidel. *The Short Story in English.* New York, 1909, 247-8.
Clarke, James Freeman. *Autobiography, Diary and Correspondence.* Edited by Edward Everett Hale. Boston and New York, 1891, 50 f., 70.
Cobb, Palmer. *The Influence of E. T. A. Hoffmann on the Tales of Edgar Allan Poe.* Chapel Hill, 1908, 5, 13, 25, 29.
Cobbe, Frances Power. *The Collected Works of Theodore Parker.* London, 1864, IX, 161-85.
Cooke, George Willis. *An Historical and Biographical Introduction to the Dial.* Prepared to accompany a reprint of "The Dial" in numbers. Cleveland, 1902, II, 184, 210 f., 225.
Conant, Helen S. *A Primer of German Literature.* New York, 1878, 193-4.
Curtis, George William. *The Correspondence of John Lothrop Motley.* New York, 1889, I, 35-6.
Desczyk, Gerhard. *Amerika in der Phantasie deutscher Dichter. Deutsch-Amerikanische Geschichtsblätter.* Jahrbuch der Deutsch-Amerikanischen Historischen Gesellschaft von Illinois, Jahrgang 1924-1925 (vol. XXIV-XXV), 50.
Doren, Mark van. *Nathaniel Hawthorne.* (*The American Men of Letters Series*). ((cop.) 1949), 138-9.
Dwight, Benjamin W. *The History of the Descendants of John Dwight of Dedham, Mass.* New York, 1874, I, 361 f., and *passim.*
Dwight, Henry Edwin. *Travels in the North of Germany, in the Years 1825 and 1826.* New York, 1829, 361-4.
Eckermann, Johann Peter. *Gespräche mit Goethe in den letzten Jahren seines Lebens.* Leipzig, 1925, 83, 85.
Encyclopaedia Americana, edited by Francis Lieber, assisted by E. Wigglesworth and T. G. Bradford. Philadelphia, 1832, XII, 254; 1941 edition, XXVI, 617-8; 1947, XXVI, 617-18 (by Professor Jacob Wittmer Hartmann).
Evans, E. P. *Abriss der Deutschen Literatur-Geschichte.* New-York, 1869, 203-05.
Felton, C. C. (tr.) of Wolfgang Menzel. *German Literature.* Boston, 1840, 3 v.

Follen, Charles. *A Practical Grammar of the German Language.* Boston, 1828, xi.

Follen, Eliza L. Cabot (Mrs.). *The Works of Charles Follen, with a Memoir of His Life.* Boston, 1841-1842. 5 v.

Francke, Kuno. *A History of German Literature as Determined by Social Forces.* New York, (cop.) 1896, 1901, 1931, 417, 452 f., 457 f., 487.

Goedeke, Karl. *Grundriss zur Geschichte der deutschen Dichtung.* Zweite ganz neu bearbeitete Auflage. Leipzig, Dresden, Berlin, 1898, VI, 32-45.

Goodnight, Scott Holland. *German Literature in American Magazines Prior to 1846* (Bulletin of the University of Wisconsin, No. 188. Philology and Literature Series, IV, No. 1, Madison, Wisconsin, 1907) 33 f., 105 f.

Gostwick, Joseph. *German Literature.* Philadelphia, 1854, 209-11.

Gostwick, Joseph and Harrison, Robert. *Outlines of German Literature.* New York, Boston (preface) 1873, 392-400.

Haertel, Martin Henry. *German Literature in American Magazines 1846 to 1880* (Bulletin of the University of Wisconsin No. 263. Philology and Literature Series, IV, No. 2, Madison, Wisconsin, 1908) 92 f.

Hatfield, James Taft. *New Light on Longfellow with Special Reference to His Relations to Germany.* Boston and New York, 1933, 58, 62 ff., 160, 162, 176.

Hatfield, James Taft. *Four Lectures* (Original and in Translation) Given at German Universities in February, 1936, Evanston, 1936. 'IV. Longfellow, A Transmitter of German Culture,' 100 f.

Hawthorne, Julian. *Nathaniel Hawthorne and His Wife.* A Biography. Boston and New York, 1889, I, 185, 192.

Higginson, Thomas Wentworth. *American Men of Letters, Margaret Fuller Ossoli.* Boston and New York, (cop. 1884), "Country Life at Groton. (1833-1836)," 45.

Hillard, George. *Life, Letters and Journals of George Ticknor.* Boston, 1876. 2 v.

Hofacker, Erich P. *German Literature as Reflected in the German-Language Press of St. Louis Prior to 1898* (Washington University Studies —New Series, Language and Literature—No. 16) St. Louis, 1946, 41 f., 110 f., and *passim.*

Hosmer, James K. *A Short History of German Literature.* Second Edition. St. Louis, 1879, 493-5, 583 f.

Howe, M. A. De Wolfe. *The Life and Letters of George Bancroft.* New York, 1908, I, 97 f.

Jenkins, William Sumner. *Pro-Slavery Thought in the Old South.* Chapel Hill, 1935, 39-40, 205, 206.

Johnson, Carl L. *Professor Longfellow of Harvard.* University of Oregon, Eugene, 1944, 47.

Joseph, Myrtle J. *Tieck and Hawthorne.* M. A. Thesis, Columbia University, 1911, 56, 58, 59.

Just, Walter. *Die romantische Bewegung in der amerikanischen Literatur: Brown, Poe, Hawthorne. Ein Beitrag zur Geschichte der Romantik.* Berlin, 1910, 38-45.

Klenze, Camillo von. *Charles Timothy Brooks*, Translator from the German and the Genteel Tradition. Boston, London, 1937, 2, 3, 16, 49.
Köpke, Rudolf. *Ludwig Tieck. Erinnerungen aus dem Leben des Dichters.* Leipzig, 1855, II, 72.
Lathrop, George Parsons. *A Study of Hawthorne.* Boston, 1876, 207.
Legaré, Hugh Swinton. *Writings of Hugh Swinton Legaré.* Prefaced by a Memoir of his Life. Edited by his Sister. Charleston, 1846, I, 139, 140 f.
Long, Orie W. *Literary Pioneers: Early American Explorers of European Culture.* Cambridge, 1935.
Long, O. W. *Frederic Henry Hedge.* A Cosmopolitan Scholar. Portland, Maine, 1940, 19, 24.
Longchamp, F. C. *Manuel du Bibliophile Français (1470-1920).* Paris et Lausanne, 1927, II.
Lüdeke, Heinrich. *Ludwig Tieck und das alte englische Theater.* Ein Beitrag zur Geschichte der Romantik. Frankfurt-am-Main, 1922, 30 f.
Matenko, Percy. *Tieck and Solger.* The Complete Correspondence. New York, Berlin, 1933.
Mathews, Albert. *Memorial of Bernard Roelker.* New-York, 1889, 4-14 (*passim*), 27.
Morgan, Bayard Quincy. *A Critical Bibliography of German Literature in English Translation, 1481-1927*, with Supplement Embracing the Years 1928-1935. Second Edition. Stanford University, California, London, 1938, 483 f.
Owen, John (pub. of tr.). *Henry of Ofterdingen: A Romance. From the German of Novalis, (Friedrich von Hardenberg).* Cambridge, 1842.
Parrington, Vernon Louis. *Main Currents in American Thought.* New York, (cop. 1927, 1930), II, 114 f.
Pattee, Fred Lewis. "The Shadow of Longfellow" (*Side-Lights on American Literature.* New York, 1922), 210-249.
Pattee, Fred Lewis. *The Development of the American Short Story.* An Historical Survey. New York and London, 1923, 102 f., 129, 292 f.
Perkins, Frederick B. *Devil-Puzzlers and Other Studies.* New York, 1877, xvi-xvii.
Perry, T. S. *Life and Letters of Francis Lieber.* Boston, 1882, 180 f.
Pierce, Frederick E.; Schreiber, Carl F. *Fiction and Fantasy of German Romance*, Selections from the German Romantic Authors, 1790-1830 (in English Translation). New York, 1927, 8, 9 f.
Quinn, Arthur Hobson. *Edgar Allan Poe.* A Critical Biography. New York, London, 1941, 289.
Spindler, George Washington. *Karl Follen.* A Biographical Study. Chicago. 1917, 96 f., 140 f.
Stedman, Edmund Clarence; Woodberry, George Edward. *Edgar Allan Poe.* New York, I (cop. 1894), cv, cix; X (cop. 1895) xxxi.
Ticknor, George. *History of Spanish Literature.* New York, 1849, 3 v.
Wade, Mason. *Margaret Fuller Whetstone of Genius.* New York, 1940, 32, 37 f.
Weber, Paul C. *America in Imaginative German Literature in the First Half of the Nineteenth Century.* New York, 1926, 51 f.

Wells, Benjamin W. *Modern German Literature*. Boston, 1897, second edition revised and enlarged, Boston, 1906, Boston, 1909, 313-14.
Whipple, E. P. *Recollections of Eminent Men*. Boston (cop. 1886), 274.
Williams, Stanley T. *The Life of Washington Irving*. New York, London, 1935, I, 179 f., 231; II, 287 f.
Wolle, Francis. *Fitz James O'Brien, a Literary Bohemian of the Eighteen-Fifties* (University of Colorado Studies, Series B. Studies in the Humanities, Vol. 2, No. 2, Boulder, May, 1944) 174, 262.
Zeydel, Edwin H. *Ludwig Tieck and England. A Study in the Literary Relations of Germany and England During the Early Nineteenth Century*. Princeton, 1931.
Zeydel, Edwin H. *Ludwig Tieck, The German Romanticist. A Critical Study*. Princeton, 1935.
Zylstra, Henry. *E. T. A. Hoffmann in England and America*. Harvard dissertation, unpublished. 1940.

B. Articles

Alewyn, Richard. "Wackenroders Anteil." *The Germanic Review*, XIX (1944), 52-58.
"American Humor." *The United States Magazine and Democratic Review*, XVII (September, 1845), 216.
"American Works of Fiction" (contains a review of Hawthorne's *Twice Told Tales*). *The Foreign and Colonial Quarterly Review*, II (October, 1843), 486, 487.—reprinted in *Littell's Living Age*, II, (October 19, 1844), 654.
Bancroft, George. "German Literature." *The American Quarterly Review*, IV (Philadelphia, 1828), 180-81.
Bancroft, George. Review of Dwight's *Travels in the North of Germany, in the Years 1825 and 1826*. *The American Quarterly Review*, VI (Philadelphia, 1829), 198-9.
Belden, Henry Marvin. "Poe's Criticism of Hawthorne." *Anglia*, XXIII (1901), 376-404.
Francke, Kuno. "Emerson and German Personality." *The International Quarterly*, VIII (September-December, 1903), 97.
Gruener, Gustav. "Poe's Knowledge of German." *Modern Philology*, II (1904), 140.
Gruener, Gustav. "Notes on the Influence of E. T. A. Hoffmann upon Edgar Allan Poe." *PMLA*, XIX, New Series XII (1904), 1-25.
Hewett-Thayer, Harvey W. "Tieck's Novellen and Contemporary Journalistic Criticism." *The Germanic Review*, III, 4 (October, 1928), 328-60.
Higginson, Thomas Wentworth. "Cheerful Yesterdays. VI. The Birth of a Literature." *The Atlantic Monthly*, LXXIX (April, 1897), 490.
Huebener, Theodore. "The First German Grammar and Reader for American Schools." *The German Quarterly*, XXII (March, 1949), 100.
Jantz, Harold S. "Samuel Miller's Survey of German Literature, 1803." *The Germanic Review*, XVI (1941), 277.
Jantz, Harold S. "German Thought and Literature in New England, 1620-1820, A Preliminary Survey." *The Journal of English and Germanic Philology*, XLI (1942), 3-4, 43, 45.

Kern, Alfred A. "The Sources of Hawthorne's *Feathertop*," *PMLA*, XLVI (December, 1931), 1253-1259.
Kern, Alfred A. "Hawthorne's *Feathertop* and R. L. R." *PMLA*, LII, (June, 1937), 503-510.
"Nathaniel Hawthorne." *The United States Magazine and Democratic Review*, XVI (April, 1845), 384.
"Nathaniel Hawthorne." *Littell's Living Age*, XXXIII (April 3, 1852), 19 (reprinted from the *New Monthly Magazine and Humorist*, vol. 94, 1852), 207.
Pochmann, Henry A. "Irving's German Sources in *The Sketch Book*." *Studies in Philology*, XXVII, No. 3 (July, 1930), 480.
Pochmann, Henry A. "Irving's German Tour and its Influence on his Tales." *PMLA*, XLV, No. 4 (December, 1930), 1150-1187.
Poe, Edgar Allan. Review of Hawthorne's *Twice-Told Tales*. *Graham's Lady's and Gentleman's Magazine*, XX (May, 1842), 298-300.
Poe, Edgar Allan. "Tale-Writing—Nathaniel Hawthorne." (Review of Hawthorne's *Twice-Told Tales* and *Mosses from an Old Manse*) *Godey's Magazine and Lady's Book*, XXXV (November, 1847), 252-256.
Review of Ludwig Tieck's: "The Life of a Poet." *Blackwood's Edinburgh Magazine*, XLII (September, 1837), 394-404.
Review of Hawthorne's *Mosses from an old Manse*. *The Athenaeum*, No. 980 (August 8, 1846) 807.
Schönbach, Anton. "Beiträge zur Charakteristik Nathaniel Hawthorne's." *Englische Studien*, VII (1884), 301-02.
Turner, Arlin. "Hawthorne's Literary Borrowings." *PMLA*, LI (June, 1936), 559.
Wagner, Lydia Elizabeth. "The Reserved Attitude of the Early German Romanticists toward America." *The German Quarterly*, XVI (January, 1943), 8.
Wahr, Fred B. "Emerson and the Germans." *Monatshefte für Deutschen Unterricht*, XXXIII (February, 1941), 49-63.
Zeydel, Edwin H. "George Ticknor and Ludwig Tieck." *PMLA*, XLIV (1929), 879-891.
Zeydel, Edwin H. "Washington Irving and Ludwig Tieck." *PMLA*, XLVI (1931), 946-947.

INDEX

A

Abbeville, Sanson d', 104.
Achenwall, D. G., 98.
Acosta, Joseph de, 98.
Acrelius, Isreal, 99.
Adams, John Quincy, 1, 11, 93.
Aeschylus, 14.
Alcott, Amos Bronson, 65.
Alewyn, Richard, 34, 114.
Alfieri, (Count) Vittorio, 65.
Allston, Wash., 97.
Alterton, Margaret, 72, 110.
Andersen, Hans Christian, 61.
Ariosto, Lodovico, 65.
Aristophanes, 14, 22, 45, 68.
Arndt, Ernst Moritz, 49.
Arnim, Achim von, 16, 27, 28, 29.
Arnim, Bettina von, 19, 54, 55.
Asher, A., 23, 92.
Austin, Sarah, 38, 108.

B

Baginsky, Paul H., 110.
Bancroft, George, 1-4, 8, 10, 92, 110, 112, 114.
Barba, Preston A., 110.
Bartlett, J. R., 97.
Baskerville, Alfred, 44, 47, 108.
Baudissin, Wolf Heinrich (Count) von, 35, 46.
Beaumont, Francis, 68.
Beck, C., 17, 32.
Beers, Henry A., 67, 72, 77, 110.
Belden, Henry Marvin, 72-75, 79, 80, 81, 87, 114.
Benecke, Georg Friedrich, 2.
Boccaccio, Giovanni, 40, 50, 51.
Bodmer, Johann Jakob, 2.
Bokum, Herman, 31, 43, 107.
Bordone, Benedetto, 99.
Bouchette, J., 99.
Bouterwek, Friedrich, 2, 3, 110.
Boyer, P., 99.
Boyesen, Hjalmar Hjorth, 13, 25, 26, 27, 28, 94, 110.
Bradford, T. G., 111.
Brandes, Edvard, 35.
Braun, Frederick Augustus, 64, 110.
Brentano, Clemens, 27, 29, 64.
Brockhaus, F. A., 23.
Brooks, Charles Timothy, 39, 47, 61, 62, 93, 111, 113.
Brooks, Van Wyk, 49, 72, 111.
Bryant, W. C., 97.
Bülow, Baron Eduard von, 5-6.

Bürger, Gottfried August, 48, 56, 87.
Büttner, Joh. Carl, 99.
Bulwer-Lytton of Knebworth, Lord Edward George, 28.
Buxton, Th. F., 106.
Byron, Lord George Gordon Noél, 29.

C

Calderón de la Barca, Pedro, 14.
Calvert, George H., 16, 111.
Cameron, Kenneth Walter, 111.
Campanius, Thom., 99.
Campbell, Killis, 72, 111.
Canby, Henry Seidel, 81, 111.
Carlyle, Thomas, 14, 15, 17, 34, 35, 42, 43, 46, 47, 53, 55, 61, 64, 78, 94, 108.
Cervantes Saavedra, Miguel de, 2, 3, 7, 14, 25, 32, 35, 45, 51, 93.
Chamisso, Adalbert, 56.
Channing, Wil. E., 97.
Channing, William Henry, 109.
Chaucer, Geoffrey, 50, 51, 69.
Chevalier, Robert, 102.
Clarke, James Freeman, 64, 65, 93, 109, 111.
Cobb, Palmer, 71, 72, 73, 111.
Cobbe, Frances Power, 111.
Colombo, Fernand., 99.
Columbus, Christopher, 90.
Conant, Helen S., 35, 111.
Cooke, George Willis, 61, 111.
Cooper, James Fenimore, 8, 10, 28, 52, 53, 91, 95, 97, 109.
Cortes, Fern., 100.
Craig, Hardin, 72, 110.
Crayon, Geoffrey, 109.
Cunningham, G. G., 108.
Curtis, George William, 111.

D

Dana, Richard Henry, 53.
Dänzer, Carl, 28.
Dante Alighieri, 6, 7, 65, 93.
Danton, Georges, 91.
Davila, Gil Gonzales, 100.
Desczyk, Gerhard, 111.
De Vries, I., 33.
De Vries, S., 105.
Doren, Mark van, 111.
Dumas, Alexandre, père, 29.

Dunn, John, 100.
Dwight, Benjamin W., 111.
Dwight, Henry Edwin, 1, 4, 5, 92, 93, 111, 114.
Dwight, Timothy, 4.

E

Ebeling, Chr. D., 100.
Eckermann, Johann Peter, 23-24, 111.
Einstein, Albert, 96.
Eliot, Thomas Stearns, 96.
Ellet, (Mrs.) E. F., 18, 41, 42.
Emerson, Edward Waldo, 109.
Emerson, Ralph Waldo, 19, 53-56, 65, 95, 109, 114, 115.
Erasmus, Desiderius (Gerhard Gerhards), 69.
Euripides, 45.
Evans, E. P., 33, 34, 111.
Everett, Edward, 1, 64.

F

Fehling, Jürgen, 34, 68.
Feiling, C. A., 44, 108.
Felton, C. C., 32, 60, 61, 111.
Fichte, Johann Gottlieb, 18, 55.
Finkenstein, Countess, 7, 8.
Fiske, Willard, 43, 46, 47, 108.
Fletcher, John, 22, 68.
Follen, Charles, 1, 10, 11, 30, 31, 39, 62, 64, 93, 107, 112, 113.
Follen, (Mrs.) Eliza L. Cabot, 112.
Forbes, Waldo Emerson, 109.
Fouqué, Friedrich de la Motte-, 16, 19, 25, 48, 76, 80.
Franciscus, Erasm., 100.
Francke, Kuno, 13, 29, 36, 43, 55, 94, 108, 112, 114.
Franklin, Benjamin, 91, 92.
Frederick William IV (King of Prussia), 23, 60, 68.
Fremont, J. C., 100.
Fuller, Margaret, 1, 11, 19, 54, 64-67, 78, 93, 95, 109, 110, 113.

G

Gervinus, Georg Gottfried, 18.
Goedeke, Karl, 72, 112.
Goethe, Ottilie, 7, 8.
Goethe, Johann Wolfgang, 2, 6, 7, 13, 14, 17-19, 22-25, 27-29, 33, 37, 44, 53, 55, 57, 61, 63-66, 76, 78, 79, 93, 108, 110, 111.

Goodnight, Scott Holland, 13, 15, 20, 38, 112.
Gostwick, Joseph, 34, 112.
Gottfriedt, Joh. Ludw., 100.
Gräter, Francis, 59.
Gray, Fr. C., 100.
Grillparzer, Franz, 25.
Grimm, Brothers, 33, 48, 56.
Gruener, Gustav, 71, 72, 114.
Grund, Leopold, 60.

H

Haertel, Martin Henry, 13, 24, 112.
Hahn-Hahn, Countess Ida, 20.
Happelius, E. G., 101.
Harrison, James A., 110.
Harrison, Robert, 34, 112.
Hartmann, Hans, 54.
Hartmann, J. A., 101.
Hartmann, Jacob Wittmer, 111.
Hatfield, James Taft, 57, 59, 112.
Hauff, Wilhelm, 20, 29, 44.
Haven, Walter, 10, 16, 17, 92.
Hawthorne, Julia, 79, 112.
Hawthorne, Nathaniel, 51, 67, 69, 71-88, 94, 95, 109, 111-115.
Hedge, Frederic Henry, 2, 15, 25, 42, 43, 45, 46, 54, 64, 108, 113.
Hegel, Georg Wilhelm Friedrich, 55.
Heine, Heinrich, 16, 17, 26, 28, 35.
Heinrich von Veldeke, 2.
Heinse, Wilhelm, 33.
Hellman, George S., 109.
Hennepin, L., 101.
Herder, Johann Gottfried, 11, 16, 19, 53, 61.
Hesselius, Andreas, 101.
Hewett-Thayer, Harvey W., 94, 114.
Heyse, Paul, 29.
Higginson, Thomas Wentworth, 1, 72, 112, 114.
Hillard, George, 112.
Hinton, J. H., 101.
Hitchcock, E., 101.
Hofacker, Erich P., 21, 29, 112.
Hoffmann, C. F., 98.
Hoffmann, E. T. A., 16, 20, 21, 27, 28, 44, 48, 49, 52, 56, 57, 59, 70, 71, 72, 75, 76, 86, 88, 111, 114.
Holberg, Ludwig, 22.
Holtei, Karl von, 10, 29, 107.
Horn, Franz, 3.
Hosmer, James K., 35, 94, 112.
Howard, William G., 43, 108.
Howe, M. A. de Wolfe, 112.
Huebener, Theodore, 30, 114.
Hughes, Griffith, 101.

INDEX

Hugo, Victor Marie, 29.
Hutson, C. W., 24.

I
Iffland, August Wilhelm, 31.
Immermann, Karl Lebrecht, 24.
Inga, Ath., 101.
Irving, Washington, 8, 10, 28, 48-52, 69, 74, 95, 98, 109, 114, 115.

J
Jacob, Therese von, 92.
Jantz, Harold S., 114.
Jean Paul, cf. Richter, J. P. F.
Jenkins, William Sumner, 90, 112.
Johnson, Carl L., 63, 112.
Jones, George, 98, 102.
Jonson, Ben, 22.
Joseph, Myrtle J., 81, 112.
Joyce, James, 96.
Julius, N. H., 6.
Just, Walter, 80, 81, 112.

K
Kant, Immanuel, 55.
Kemble, John, 68, 69.
Kern, Alfred A., 80, 83, 85, 86, 115.
Kleist, Heinrich von, 49.
Klenze, Camillo von, 62, 113.
Klopstock, Friedrich Gottlieb, 11.
Koch, Erduin Julius, 26.
Köpke, Rudolf, 46, 113.
Körner, Theodor, 65.
Kosciusco, Thaddäus, 91, 92.
Kotzebue, August von, 31, 45.

L
Lafontaine, August Heinrich Julius, 19.
Lahontan, Bar. de, 102.
Lathrop, George Parsons, 86, 87, 109, 113.
Le Blanc, Vincent., 102.
Legaré, Hugh Swinton, 8, 9, 113.
Leibnitz, Gottfried Wilhelm Freiherr von, 102.
Leiste, Ch., 102.
Leon, J. Ponce de, 102.
Le Sage, Alain René, 102.
Lescarbot, Marc., 102.
Leslie, Miss, 74.

Lessing, Gotthold Ephraim, 11, 16, 19, 65.
Lieber, Francis, 6, 9, 92, 111, 113.
Long, J., 102.
Long, Orie, W., 113.
Longchamp, F. C., 73, 113.
Longfellow, Henry Wadsworth, 32, 33, 41, 56-64, 69, 79, 93-95, 109, 112, 113.
Longfellow, Samuel, 58, 110.
Lorrain, Claude (Claude Gelée), 58, 59.
Louis XIV, 47.
Lowell, James Russell, 67-69, 75, 80, 95, 110.
Ludewig, H. E., 103.
Lüdeke, Heinrich, 113.
Lüttichau, Ida von, 6.
Lüttichau, Wolf Adolf von, 4.
Luther, Martin, 54.

M
Maffei, J. P., 103.
Manzoni, (Count) Alessandro, 65.
Marquard, Joh., 103.
Marquette, P. & Joliet, 103.
Martin, Robert Montgomery, 103.
Matenko, Percy, 113.
Matheson, J., 104.
Mathews, Albert, 113.
Menzel, Wolfgang, 32, 49, 111.
Mesqua, Mira de, 7.
Meyer, H. L., 100.
Miller, Samuel, 114.
Minor, J., 36.
Mirabeau, (Count) Honoré de, 91.
Mörike, Eduard, 24.
Montaigne, Michel Eyquem Seigneur de, 53.
Montanus, Arnold, 103.
Morgan, Bayard Quincy, 72, 113.
Motley, John Lothrop, 7, 8, 10, 39, 40, 41, 49, 92, 93, 111.
Mozart, Wolfgang Amadeus, 41.
Mühlbach, Luise (Clara Mundt), 25.
Mulready, John, 60.
Musaeus, Johann Karl August, 47, 108.

N
Neal, Daniel, 103.
Nicolai, Friedrich, 26, 31.
Norton, Charles Eliot, 109.

Novalis (Friedrich von Hardenberg), 16, 17, 18, 27, 29, 32, 36, 49, 55, 56, 61, 65, 76.

O

O'Brien, Fitz James, 69, 70, 95, 110, 114.
Oehlenschläger, Adam Gottlob, 48.
Osgood, Mrs., 20, 21.
Owen, John, 32, 113.
Oxenford, John, 108.

P

Parker, Theodore, 19, 111.
Parrington, Vernon Louis, 113.
Pattee, Fred Lewis, 63, 64, 78, 113.
Paulding, J. K., 106.
Peabody, Elizabeth, 79, 87.
Peabody, Sophia, 79, 87.
Pearson, Norman Holmes, 79.
Perkins, Frederick B., 76, 113.
Perry, T. S., 113.
Petrarca, Francesco, 65.
Philalethes [King John of Saxony (1801-1873)], 5, 6.
Pierce, Frederick E., 63, 113.
Pizarro y Orllana, D. Fr., 103.
Pochmann, Henry A., 49, 50, 51, 115.
Poe, Edgar Allan, 69, 71-81, 86, 95, 110-115.
Prescott, W. H., 104.
Priest, William, 104.

Q

Quinn, Arthur Hobson, 71, 113.

R

Ramsay, David, 104.
Raumer, Friedrich von, 6, 15.
Reed, A., 104.
Richter, Jean Paul Friedrich, 11, 17, 19, 28, 35, 44, 47-49, 51, 53, 55-57, 63-65, 108.
Robertson, William, 104.
Robespierre, Maximilien de, 91.
Robinson, Edward, 8, 92.
Robinson, Henry Crabb, 61.
Roelker, Bernard, 32, 33, 59, 107, 113.
Rogers, Richard S., 86.
Rosenstengel, W. H., 35, 108.
Rousseau, J. J., 33, 36.
Rusk, Ralph L., 54, 109.

S

Sand, George (Aurore Dupin, Baroness Dudevant), 29.
Schelling, Friedrich Wilhelm, 18, 19, 35, 53, 54, 55.
Scherer, H., 104.
Schiller, Friedrich, 11, 13, 15-19, 23, 24, 55, 63-65, 108.
Schlegel, August Wilhelm, 3, 7-9, 17-19, 24, 32, 33, 46, 54, 59, 61, 63, 107.
Schlegel, Friedrich, 3, 18, 19, 24, 29, 32, 33, 49, 53, 54, 55, 61, 63.
Schlosser, Friedrich, 54.
Schmitt, G. A., 11, 30.
Schönbach, Anton, 81, 86, 88, 115.
Schreiber, Carl F., 63, 113.
Schröder, Friedrich Ludwig, 61.
Scott, Walter, 48, 52.
Sealsfield, Charles (Karl Anton Postl), 28.
Shakespeare, William, 3-9, 14-16, 22-24, 26, 32, 34, 35, 45, 68, 69, 93.
Shelley, Mrs., 52.
Sloane, Hans, 104.
Smith, Jane Browning, 58, 60, 108.
Smith, John, 104.
Solger, Karl Wilhelm Ferdinand, 28, 54, 56, 113.
Sophocles, 14, 19, 45.
Soto, Ferd. de., 105.
Spielhagen, Friedrich, 29.
Spindler, Karl, 1, 20, 29.
St. Mery, Moreau de, 103.
Staël, Germaine de, 64.
Stedman, Edmund Clarence, 76, 113.
Steffens, Henrik, 18.
Sterne, Lawrence, 33.
Stewart, Randall, 77, 79, 82, 109.
Swinburne, Algernon Charles, 67.

T

Tasso, Torquato, 65.
Ternaux-Compans, H., 105.
Thatcher, B. B., 105.
Thoreau, Henry David, 67, 83, 95, 110.
Thümmel, Moritz August von, 33.
Ticknor, George, 1, 5, 6, 7, 9, 10, 52, 56, 61, 64, 92, 93, 112, 113, 115.
Tieck, Dorothea, 35, 46.
Tieck, Friedrich, 6.
Trent, William P., 109.
Tucker, G., 105.
Turner, Arlin, 76, 115.

U

Uhland, Ludwig, 36, 57, 63, 64, 95.
Ulloa, D. Ant. de, 105.
Ulloa, D. Jorge Juan de, 105.
Ungern-Sternberg, Baron von, 5.

V

Vega, Lope de, 7, 51.
Villagutierrez de Soto Mayor, Juan de, 105.

W

Wackenroder, Wilhelm Heinrich, 26, 27, 33, 34, 47, 54, 61, 64, 89, 107, 108, 114.
Wade, Mason, 113.
Wagner, Lydia Elizabeth, 89, 115.
Wahr, Fred B., 53, 54, 55, 115.
Ward, Samuel, 59.
Warner, Charles Dudley, 108.
Washington, George, 91, 92.
Weber, Paul C., 113.
Webster, Noah, 98.
Weld, Isaac, 105.
Wells, Benjamin W., 36-37, 94, 114.
Wheeler, Charles Stearns, 19, 54.
Whipple, E. P., 7, 114.
Wieland, Christoph Martin, 11, 19, 28, 35, 48, 53.
Wigglesworth, E., 111.
Wilder, Thornton, 96.
Williams, Stanley T., 48, 51, 114.
Winckelmann, Johann Joachim, 53, 54.
Wolf, Friedrich August, 60.
Wolle, Francis, 114.
Woodberry, George Edward, 76, 113.

Z

Zeydel, Edwin H., 1, 4, 5, 6, 7, 9, 10, 15, 16, 23, 26, 39, 42, 44, 45, 46, 51, 52, 54, 60, 87, 94, 114, 115.
Zorgdrager, C. G., 105.
Zschokke, Heinrich, 20, 29, 59, 76.
Zylstra, Henry, 52, 69, 71, 75, 79, 88, 114.

www.ingramcontent.com/pod-product-compliance
Lightning Source LLC
Chambersburg PA
CBHW031317150426
43191CB00005B/263